William Duncan Thomson

The Christian Miracles and the Conclusions of Science

William Duncan Thomson

The Christian Miracles and the Conclusions of Science

ISBN/EAN: 9783743346475

Manufactured in Europe, USA, Canada, Australia, Japa

Cover: Foto ©Lupo / pixelio.de

Manufactured and distributed by brebook publishing software (www.brebook.com)

William Duncan Thomson

The Christian Miracles and the Conclusions of Science

HANDBOOKS

FOR

BIBLE CLASSES

AND PRIVATE STUDENTS.

EDITED BY

REV. MARCUS DODS, D.D.,

AND

REV. ALEXANDER WHYTE, D.D.

THE CHRISTIAN MIRACLES.
BY REV. W. D. THOMSON, M.A.

PRINTED BY MORRISON AND GIBB,

FOR

T. & T. CLARK, EDINBURGH,

LONDON, . HAMILTON, ADAMS, AND CO.
DUBLIN, . GEORGE HERBERT.
NEW YORK, . SCRIBNER AND WELFORD

THE

CHRISTIAN MIRACLES

AND THE

CONCLUSIONS OF SCIENCE.

BY

REV. W. D. THOMSON, M.A.

CONTENTS.

---o---

CHAP.		PAGES
I.	INTRODUCTION.—THE SUPERNATURAL,	9-19

The Object of Inquiry. Supernaturalism in Danger—The Danger exists in various Quarters—Its Sources—It involves Danger to Spiritual Life—The Supernatural in its Technical Sense. Supernatural Action defined: Questions involved—The Impossibility of exact Definition—Supernatural Power is above Nature—This Power acts within Nature—It does not act unnaturally—(1) It does not act independently of Means—(2) It conforms to the Law of Cause and Effect—(3) It introduces no Disorder among Natural Forces.

II.	MIRACLES DEFINED.—THE BIBLE,	20-25

The Term Miracle. Exact Definition required. How the Bible regards Miracles. The Miracles as Wonders: The Value of the Feeling of Wonder—Christ took advantage of this Feeling. The Miracles as Signs: Why they were called Signs—Their Value as Signs—Why they were necessary as Signs. The Miracles as Powers: General Meaning of the Term Power—There are various Kinds of Power according to the Bible and Science—It was to be expected that Christ would do mighty Works.

III.	MIRACLES DEFINED.—NATURE,	25-33

Science rendering Definition of Miracles more easy. What is Nature: Nature difficult to define—Huxley's Definition. New Definition of Miracles. Other Definitions: Locke's Definition examined—Hume's Definition and his Argument examined—C. Hodge's Definition examined—Westcott's Definition examined. The new Definition and Science: The Definition and the Principle of Design—The Definition and God's Immanence in Nature—The Definition and ordinary Exercises of His Power in Nature—The Definition and extraordinary Exercises of His Power—Science bound to admit Innovations of Power in Nature.

IV.	GOD'S RELATION TO NATURE.—SCIENCE,	34-41

The Question as to God's Relation to Nature necessary. Mode of Treatment. The Province of Science: God's Relation to Nature not a matter for Science to settle—Why so?—The Duty of Science as to Religious Questions. Science a Transgressor in causing Religious Doubt. Qualifications: In many instances Religion and Science deal with the same Subjects—Science helps to enlarge Conceptions of God—Science in its Discoveries is on the side of Teleology—Science tends to make Religion exact in its Knowledge—Science by its Faith in Matter is committed to Faith in Miracle.

CHAP.		PAGES
V.	GOD'S RELATION TO NATURE.—RELIGION,	42-52

This a Question for Religion. Biblical Theory defined. Biblical Theory examined: The Parts of it to be kept in view—The Wisdom of the Theory—The Theory a Proof of Divine Revelation—It implies the Possibility of Miracles—The Religion of Scripture Supernatural. Agnosticism: It has no Religious Beliefs—It has no Speculative Theory— Its Connection with Science is incidental. Positivism: Positivism defined—Its Relation to the Supernatural. Rationalism: Rationalism defined — Rationalism and Deism—Rationalism and the Miraculous—Rationalism and Reason, Scripture, Science, Speculation, Religion, Morality.

| VI. | GOD'S RELATION TO NATURE.—EVOLUTION, | 53 68 |

Evolution does not exclude the Possibility of Miracles. Evolution a Speculation. A Study of Evolution called for in the Interest of Miracles. The Scope of Evolution. Six general Principles of Evolution. Evidence in favour of Evolution: A large Mass of Evidence seems to favour it—This Evidence does not verify it—All the Evidence is likewise in favour of Creationism. Evidence against Evolution: Evolution depends on the Principle of Continuity—It does not fulfil the Requirements of this Principle—What are Difficulties to Evolution are not such to Creationism. Miracles and Evolution as supposed verified: Evolution and Materialism, Agnosticism, and God's Immanence in Nature—Continuity defined.—As so defined, it is consistent with Miracles.

| VII. | GOD'S RELATION TO NATURE.—CONTINUITY, | 69-77 |

Continuity explained: Importance of Continuity as a Principle—The Principle capable of many Applications—Continuity and its Relation to Power. Continuity and Miracles: Continuity and a Spiritual World—Continuity and a Personal God—Continuity and God as an Efficient Cause in Nature—Continuity and Special Acts of Creation. Special Acts of Creation defined—Special Acts of Creation consistent with Continuity. Continuity consistent with Miracles. Miracles and "The Unseen Universe:" Object of the Book—Quotations—Possibility of Miracles reconciled with Continuity — Miracles and the energy of the Unseen Universe.

| VIII. | MIRACLES AND NATURAL LAW, | 78-88 |

Natural Law not Natural Force. All Natural Laws have common Features. What is Natural Law?—(1) Natural Law depends on Natural Force—(2) Laws of Nature vary with the Forces of Nature, etc.—(3) No Natural Law is in any sense a Natural Force—(4) Natural Laws not Entities in Nature—(5) There can be no Natural Law for a Single Event. Miracles and the Definition: The Definition strictly Scientific—The Christian Miracles consistent with all the Five Elements of the Definition. What about Natural Force?

CHAP.		PAGES
IX.	MIRACLES AND NATURAL LAWS,	89–99

The Question of Miracles and the Laws of Nature. Miracles and *general* Laws of Nature: (1) The Christian Miracles fulfil the Law of Efficient Causation—(2) They fulfil the Law of Final Causation—(3) They fulfil the Law of the Persistence of the Action of Force—(4) They fulfil the Law of combined Action among Forces—(5) They fulfil the Law according to which higher Forces unite in action with lower ones—(6) They fulfil the Law according to which the Action of one Force modifies that of another. Miracles and particular Groups of Natural Law: The Christian Miracles cannot be classified under such Laws—They were singular Events—Yet absolutely consistent with all such Laws.

X.	MIRACLES AND NATURAL FORCE,	100–109

The Question stated. What Natural Force is not: (1) Natural Force not Spiritual Force—(2) Natural Force not a Scientific Principle—(3) Natural Force not the Effects of its Action. What Natural Force is: (1) All Natural Force exists in connection with Matter—(2) It is distinguished by Science from Matter—(3) Natural Force revealed as Power to Act, and as Power to receive Action—(4) Energy may be Latent as well as Active. The Conclusions and the Christian Miracles.

XI.	MIRACLES AND THE INCAPABILITIES OF NATURAL FORCE,	110–119

Introduction. Natural Force is Inscrutable: Science finds Natural Force mysterious—The Fundamental Questions of Religion and Science—The Inscrutability of Natural Force examined—Its Application to the Christian Miracles. Natural Force is Indestructible: The Law of the Conservation of Energy defined—The Bearing of the Law on the Christian Miracles. Natural Force is incapable of Self-existence: All Natural Force Relative and Dependent—Materialism disproved. The Power on which Natural Force depends: (1) This Power must be held to be Absolute, etc.—This Conclusion pointed to by Science—This View and Miracles—(2) This Power as a Person: Religion and Philosophy—This View and the Miracles—(3) What if it is uncertain whether or not the Power is Personal: Herbert Spencer—This View and Miracles.

XII.	MIRACLES AND THE CAPABILITIES OF NATURAL FORCE,	120–131

Introduction. Capabilities of Natural Force: (1) Four of these restated from Chap. IX., and viewed in a new Way—Miracles in accordance with them—(2) Natural Force in Action has Power to effect Change—Miracles in accordance with this—(3) Natural Force can be overcome or resisted in its Action—Miracles in accordance with this—(4) Natural Force can be aided in its Action—Miracles in accordance with this—(5) Natural Force can be transformed—Miracles in accordance with this. The Mysteries of a Drop of Water and a tiny Flame—The Lesson they teach.

CHAP.		PAGES
XIII.	THE INCARNATION POSSIBLE.—SCIENCE,	132-140

The Incarnation as a Characteristic of Christianity. The Incarnation as a striking Fact. Science has a Title to inquire into the Possibility of the Incarnation. The Incarnation and Biology: How Biology has to do with it — The Biological Question—Why Biology must admit the Possibility of the Incarnation. The Incarnation and the Biologist: An Explanation—(1) The Biologist as a Creationist and the Incarnation—(2) The Biologist as an Evolutionist and the Incarnation. The Incarnation and the Theory of Organic Evolution in General: General Statement—Groups of Salient Facts—Does the Process of Evolution continue? If so, In what direction? The Incarnation fulfils the requirements indicated.

XIV.	THE INCARNATION NECESSARY. RELIGION,	141-155

Preliminary. The Incarnation and its Metaphysical Possibility. The Incarnation and its Ethical Possibility. Mode of Inquiry as to the Necessity for it. The Incarnation and Law. The Incarnation and *Final* Causation: (1) The Incarnation and Man's Spiritual Needs—(2) The Incarnation designed to meet those needs—What is Christianity? or the true Evangelical—(3) The Incarnation a way to meet those needs. The Incarnation and Efficient Causation: God's Love as Grace required the Incarnation to give it adequate Power—God's Love leads to the Incarnation—God's Grace and Christ's Person—God's Grace and Christ's Personal History God's Grace and Christ's Self-sacrifice—God's Grace and Christ's Sufferings. Christ as the Power of God in Effect: Sin and Man's spiritual relations to God and to his brother—Christ's Power in its effect on God—Christ's Power in its effect on Man, in His character as Revealer, Reconciler, Redeemer.

XV.	THE INCARNATION VERIFIED.—RELIGION AND HISTORY,	156-169

The Nature of the Inquiry. Christ's Life as Human was spiritually Perfect: The Records of His Life—General Statements as to His spiritual Perfection—His Life as Human in its spiritual Relation to God—His Life as Human in its spiritual Relation to Men—Christ as related to Himself through His Conduct—A Qualification. Christ was the eternal Son of God: (1) His spiritual Perfection as Man proves Him to be Divine—(2) His Claim to be the Son of God, taken with His spiritual Perfection, proves His Divinity—(3) His Divinity proved by the effect of His Personality on the Mind—(4) God's Love as revealed in Him proves Him to be Divine—(5) The effect of Christ's Love in Men proves Him to be Divine.

CHAPTER I.

INTRODUCTION.—THE SUPERNATURAL.

The Object of Inquiry. Supernaturalism in Danger—The Danger exists in various Quarters—Its Sources—It involves Danger to Spiritual Life—The Supernatural in its Technical Sense. Supernatural Action defined: Questions involved—The Impossibility of exact Definition—Supernatural Power is above Nature—This Power acts within Nature—It does not act unnaturally—(1) It does not act independently of Means—(2) It conforms to the Law of Cause and Effect—(3) It introduces no Disorder among Natural Forces.

THE OBJECT OF INQUIRY.

1. The Christian miracles constitute a class of supernatural phenomena. In this Treatise the attempt is made to reconcile the possibility of their occurrence with the conclusions of science. They are not examined one by one, nor as arranged in various groups. They are considered rather as a whole, as all alike involving the action of supernatural power within the course of nature: and the attempt made is to show the compatibility of such action with the order of nature as explained by science. The Incarnation, however, is the foundation-miracle of Christianity; and the possibility of this miracle involves that of all the rest. Hence it is singled out after general conclusions have been reached; and its possibility as a Biological occurrence is vindicated.

SUPERNATURALISM IN DANGER.

2. The question of the Christian miracles and their relation to nature involves the larger question of the supernatural in general. Every form of the Christian supernatural in relation to human belief has long been on its trial, and the probation is still in process. It is held that belief in the supernatural is inconsistent with intellectual seriousness; that this belief is doomed to extinction by modern culture; and that while there is in Christianity a spiritual element which men cannot do without, the supernatural does not belong to the essence of its character and history.

3. The supernatural meets with unbelief in more forms than one. The Materialist does not admit the occurrence of supernatural action in the course of nature, because such action implies belief in the existence of a supernatural world and of a personal God. The Agnostic does not admit it, because he has hopelessly committed himself to intellectual doubt about the matter. The Positivist does not admit it, because he has persuaded himself that all the ends of human existence can be realized independently of the supernatural altogether. The Rationalist does not admit it, because while he believes in the existence of a supernatural world and of a personal God, and while he may believe in the divine omnipresence in nature, he regards all supernatural action in nature as something which is either not required or not possible. Moreover, the mental attitude of many who would decline to be classified under any of these names is one of practical unbelief; and the possibility of supernatural action in nature, or the fact of its having occurred, gives them no concern; unless, perhaps, in moments of fear for the consequences of transgression, or of desire for *post-mortem* happiness.

4. This manifold danger to supernaturalism has arisen from various sources. But there are only two which it concerns us to notice here.

In the *first* place, supernaturalism has been endangered by some of its own advocates, who have unnecessarily provoked opposition to it by making supernatural action responsible for forms of discordance with nature which have no existence in reality.

But, *secondly*, the main source of the danger has been science. The methods, the discoveries, the conclusions of science, and the practical applications of its discoveries which science has made, have all tended to weaken or to destroy the hold of the supernatural on certain minds. But this result from science has been purely incidental; and consequently it is not likely to be permanent. Science does not necessarily lead to disbelief in the fact or in the possibility of supernatural action. On the contrary, when one is satisfied that he has historical or moral grounds for believing in such action, he will find in the conclusions of science nothing incompatible with his faith, and much to confirm it. A distinction requires to be made between the actual conclusions of science, in so far as they bear upon the supernatural, and those scientific authorities who deny the supernatural. Science has its false prophets as well as religion. And what concerns those who defend supernaturalism is not the opinion of any man of science, but the testimony of science itself, as to the order of nature, and as to what it knows or does not know about it. So far as science is concerned, those who believe in the supernatural have nothing to fear, if only the distinction just indicated is kept in view, and if no misinterpretation is put upon the message that science has to deliver. Its message is worthy of all acceptation; and no one should be more ready so to accept it than he who seeks to maintain and to propagate enlightened and firm belief in the supernatural. Religion teaches us to believe in the supernatural, because it reveals to us God; and science helps us to believe in the supernatural, because it gives us a revelation of nature. If nature is not dependent upon that which is supernatural above itself, it is dependent upon that which is supernatural within itself. When nature is understood as revealed by science, the real difficulty presented is not that of believing in the supernatural, but that of escaping from such a belief.

5. The danger in which supernaturalism is involved implies a real danger to spiritual life, to spiritual religion and morality. True spiritual life, that is, life in Christ, is in some of its aspects a life truly supernatural. It is life hid with Christ in God. The man who lives this life on earth is in the natural world and the world supernatural at the same time. He is in the natural world on the organic side of his existence, and he is in the supernatural world on the side of his spirit and by his faith. There is that which is supernatural in his dependence on God, in his union and fellowship with Christ, in his prayers, in the reference of his entire life to the divine will and purpose, in his peace which passeth all understanding. Eternal life as a present life in the Christian is not a life in which he merely stands related to supernatural action that occurred many centuries ago, or that may happen in time to come. It is a life that has been begotten in him by supernatural action, and that is sustained thereby every day. The life of Abraham was a supernatural life, so was the life of Moses, so was the life of Paul, and so is the life of every man who lives by faith in God. Moreover, so long as Christ continued an object for His apostles, outwardly present with them in the natural world, their spiritual life was but poor and feeble. And it was only after He was taken up from them out of sight, and had become a supernatural object for their faith, that their spiritual life unfolded itself in such richness and power.

6. This supernatural life, then, is the true Christian life, and this life is endangered by the existing dangers in which supernaturalism is involved. What all earnest Christians are called upon to concern themselves about is not only whether Christianity is to be deprived of a supernatural character and history which belonged to it in ages long gone by, but also whether it is to be deprived of its supernatural character as a present life and power. If it is deprived of the former, it will be deprived of the latter also. If men came generally to believe, and more especially if professing

Christians came generally to believe, that no supernatural action has ever entered into the course of nature, then the Christian religion as a life hid with Christ in God, as a life of fellowship with God, as a supernatural life, would be doomed; and if any religion existed at all in the name of Christianity, it would either be only some empty form of worship, or "morality touched with emotion." The Christian for all time will require the past supernatural character and history of Christianity. He will require them to certify to him that he possesses a divine revelation and a divine Saviour, offering to him sure guidance and all-sufficient help. And he will require them as an aid to keep up his consciousness of the supernatural world, and to stimulate and strengthen his faith to live a spiritual life with reference to the divine objects and the everlasting hopes of that world.

7. To prevent ambiguity, care must be taken not to confound the supernatural, as it is involved in ordinary spiritual life, with that form of the supernatural which has been revealed in miraculous events. This latter form of the supernatural is extraordinary, and it enters the very essence of Christianity. The revelation contained in the Bible, the person of Christ, His mighty deeds, His resurrection from the dead, His ascension to heaven, the effusion of His Spirit, were results from extraordinary supernatural action within the course of nature; and it devolves on the Christian, in the interests of spiritual religion, to prove, if he can, the possibility of such action; and to prove it on scientific grounds: for it is mainly in consequence of science that it is at present denied or doubted. But if the supernatural element in Christianity is to be vindicated, and shown to be consistent with the conclusions of science, and with "intellectual seriousness" and modern culture, there are two conditions which must be fulfilled. On the one hand, the real significance of the conclusions of science must be understood, and faithfully represented; and, on the other, supernatural action in its relation to nature must not have its true character in any way exaggerated and falsified. Misunderstanding on the part of Theologians of the actual conclusions

of science and their bearings on the supernatural, and reckless and misleading definitions of the supernatural itself, are largely to blame for the opposition which religion has had to encounter from science. At present, let us make some inquiry as to the nature of supernatural action.

SUPERNATURAL ACTION DEFINED.

8. The idea of the supernatural presupposes the existence of an invisible universe and a personal God. Meanwhile, however, it is to the smaller matter of supernatural *action* alone that we turn our attention. What are the characteristics of a supernatural action as an action receiving effect in the course of nature?

9. It is evident that the supernatural requires to be defined with reference to the natural, as it is something in contrast with it. And, of course, supernatural action must be defined with special reference to those conditions in nature where, it may be supposed, such action would immediately arise. The entire question of supernatural action in its relation to the course of nature resolves itself ultimately into questions as to power or force. A supernatural action involves power; and in all supernatural action we have this power above nature, working among and in direct connection with the forces of nature below.

10. It is where their power or force lies that the supernatural and the natural come into the most direct relation to each other. And here it is that the most intelligent view is gained of how impossible it is to define the two spheres, the supernatural and the natural, so as to make it apparent even to oneself where the one ends and the other begins. And even if we could so define it, there would still remain the difficulty of understanding the manner in which supernatural action takes effect amid natural conditions. But this is not a reason why we should conclude that supernatural action has never happened in the course of nature. For we meet with the same kind of difficulty in view of the action of natural forces. These are related to each other. One force

operates along with other forces; and forces counteract each other, and modify each other in their action; and how all this takes place involves mysteries for us as dark as is the mode in which supernatural power is exercised. Let us note what appear to be some of the leading features of a supernatural action.

11. *First*, The term *super*natural implies that the power concerned in supernatural action is *above* nature. It is a power which has a transcendent existence in relation to the ordinary forces of nature. Viewed in this way, supernatural power presents two aspects as contrasted with the forces of nature. (1) It is different from the forces of nature; and (2) it is higher than the forces of nature. Observing this, then, it is impossible to see how any reasonable scientific objection can be raised to the action of supernatural power in nature. These two features of this power are both natural. The idea of one power as different from another power, and the idea of one power as higher than other powers, are both ideas which we have derived from nature. And there are no ideas of what is natural with which science is more familiar than it is with both. It knows how natural it is, moreover, for one force to work in immediate connection with other forces differing from it, and for higher forces to work in immediate connection with lower forces. And all this is in favour of the possibility of the action of supernatural power in direct connection with the forces of nature; though the power acting is not the same as any of the natural forces known to science, and though it is higher than all of them.

12. *Second*, It is a misconception of supernatural action to suppose that it must take place in an *extra*-natural way. A power transcending the system of forces in nature might be, at the same time, a power working among those forces, and even in or through them. In other words, supernatural power might act upon the course of nature, and it might give rise to extraordinary phenomena in the course of nature; and yet the action upon nature might take place from *within*, and not from without. All the supernatural occurrences referred by the Bible to the action of

divine power arose within the course of nature. They became facts in nature; and the more closely they are examined, the more does it become apparent that, while they sprang from the action of a power above nature, they yet sprang from this power as acting within natural conditions; and as acting, in particular, in immediate connection with natural forces, which act as *inner* causes of ordinary natural phenomena.

13. Consequently, we can see here what may be set down as a radical error in Bushnell's definition of the supernatural. According to him, supernatural power always acts upon nature from without. "The supernatural" he defines as "that range of substance, if any such there be, that acts upon the chain of cause and effect in nature from without the chain, producing thus results that by mere nature could not come to pass." By the chain of cause and effect is here meant, of course, the entire system of working causation in nature, and the ordinary consequences that arise from its action when not interfered with by the action of supernatural power. And the definition entirely excludes the action of supernatural power from within this system. That is to say, what are called "second causes" exist and operate independently of the divine presence and efficiency in them. In other words, the definition contains the element of *semi*-Deism. But such a definition of the supernatural cannot be accepted. Even though it could be reconciled with science, it could not be reconciled with Scripture. But it can be reconciled with neither. Science knows that second causes as implying force must be in immediate relation to some higher power on which they depend. And the Bible never wearies in testifying to the divine presence and efficiency as all-pervasive in nature. And, surely, if God is present at all in nature, He must be in it as a system of cause and effect; and if He operates at all, it must be within this system, and in direct connection with its forces. Any definition of the supernatural, fitted to meet alike the requirements of Scripture and of science, must set down this inner relation of divine power to the chain of cause and effect as one of its fundamental

principles. And this done, it becomes easy to conceive the naturalness of extraordinary supernatural events by referring them to extraordinary exercises of Divine power within the system of causation in nature.

14. *Third*, It is necessary also to define supernatural action as not being *contra*-natural action. It is not *un*natural. And yet it has often been represented by Theologians and others as bearing this character. And if there is one thing more required than another in the matter of definition, it is that the supernatural should be proved and shown on scientific grounds to be *not* ,*un*natural. If supernatural power acted in certain ways not in accordance with its actual method, it would lie open to the charge of acting unnaturally. Let us take a few instances, as they will help by way of contrast to illustrate the naturalness of the supernatural.

15. (1.) Supernatural power might be said, perhaps, to act unnaturally if it acted altogether independently of conditions and means existing in nature. But supernatural power does not act in this way, and it should not be made responsible for so acting. If we are not to reject the authority of the Bible, we must conclude that never since nature began to exist, has God exercised His power in nature in an ordinary or extraordinary manner without making some use or other of means already existing in nature. It must be remembered, of course, that the question here is entirely one with respect to the relation of the supernatural to the natural, and not one at all as to any exercise of Divine power before the natural in its pristine condition came into existence. The point of the definition put forward is, that just as science requires, so the Bible claims, that the action of supernatural power in the course of nature or upon it, ever since nature came into being, has in every instance proceeded in some way or other on the use of conditions or means already existing in nature. And so here again we are in view of another element of naturalness in the supernatural.

16. (2.) Supernatural power, again, might be charged with

acting unnaturally if it acted out of accordance with the law of cause and effect, which is so absolutely universal in nature. In Bushnell's definition there is a want of clearness as to the precise relation of the supernatural to this law. But his words suggest the idea that supernatural action and its consequences somehow transcend this law, and are incapable of explanation by reference to it. Such a view, however, can never be accepted as expressing the real truth. And in any case it is a view which science can regard only with the utmost incredulity. It knows that everything happening in nature happens in accordance with this law; and one of its conclusions is that nothing can happen anywhere or under any conditions, so as to transcend classification under it. Let Theology, then, admit that in this, science is right; and let it extend the law of cause and effect to the supernatural as absolutely as science is compelled to extend it to the natural. To do otherwise is to incur the just blame of exciting prejudice against the supernatural in the scientific mind. And to do otherwise is to degrade the supernatural, and to exalt the natural above it. For, in reality, that which is classified under the law of cause and effect, however supernatural it might be as an event, is not lowered by the fact of such a classification, but exalted. Hence we have here also an instance of the naturalness of the supernatural.

17. (3.) Let us take only one example more. Supernatural power would act unnaturally if it produced disorder among the forces of nature. Natural forces, for instance, are constant in their action; and supernatural power would act unnaturally if it destroyed this constancy. Again, some natural forces have the power of combining with others in action; and supernatural power would act unnaturally if it rendered such combination impossible. But no such disorder ever arose among the forces of nature from any exercise of Divine power amid the conditions and in connection with the forces of nature. The extraordinary action of God's power in nature no more introduced disorder or the least derangement among natural forces than does the action of any

one of those forces themselves. And here once more we see how natural, how consistent with nature, is the action of supernatural power. All is natural; all is in perfect harmony with nature. The only difference is, that the power which works supernaturally is a power different from the forces of nature, and higher in its character. And even in this there is naturalness. For there are various forces in nature and forces higher and forces lower in their order.

CHAPTER II.

MIRACLES DEFINED.—THE BIBLE.

The Term Miracle. Exact Definition required. How the Bible regards Miracles. The Miracles as Wonders: The Value of the Feeling of Wonder—Christ took advantage of this Feeling. The Miracles as Signs: Why they were called Signs—Their Value as Signs—Why they were necessary as Signs. The Miracles as Powers: General Meaning of the Term Power—There are various Kinds of Power according to the Bible and Science—It was to be expected that Christ would do mighty Works.

THE TERM MIRACLE.

18. The word *miracle* means something wonderful; some event so singular and strange as to strike the observer, and awaken the feeling of wonder in him. Hence the word, so understood, does not serve the purpose of a full and clear definition of the Christian miracles. These miracles possessed some essential features, which the meaning of the word does not include. Besides, the observant mind wonders not only in view of miracles, but also in the presence of multitudes of other phenomena in nature and events in history.

MUCH DEPENDS ON EXACT DEFINITION.

19. A true conception of the real and distinctive nature of the Christian miracles is of the utmost importance. For the want of such a conception, in many instances, not only the miracles themselves, but the Christian religion in its general character, has suffered much both from friends and foes. Moreover, it is to be

hoped with confidence that in proportion as religion and science approach each other on the line of a true definition, the Christian miracles will continue to be a glorious heritage, and an essential part of the former, while the latter will acknowledge belief in them to be consistent alike with pure religious sentiment and with the honour of the highest attainments in intellectual culture. The need for a precise definition of miracles has been well expressed by Professor Huxley. "The first step in this, as in all other discussions," he says, "is to come to a clear understanding as to the meaning of the terms employed. Argumentation whether miracles are possible, and if possible, credible, is mere beating the air until the arguers have agreed what they mean by the word 'miracle.'"

HOW THE BIBLE REGARDS MIRACLES.

20. The *Bible* defines the Christian miracles in its own way, and from its own points of view. Being exclusively a religious book, it does not set itself to define them from the standpoint of nature or science, but from the standpoint of the moral source, the moral power, the moral aim, and the moral effect which they represented. The blind received their sight, the lame walked, the lepers were cleansed, the deaf heard, the dead were raised up; and all this happened in organic connection with the Person and work of Him who had come to preach the gospel of the kingdom of God. Accordingly, in outlining its definition of these miracles, the Bible wisely selects its terms from a supreme and sole regard to religious and moral considerations; thus simply remaining silent as to all questions bearing on the relation of the miraculous to the internal arrangements, forces, and laws of nature.

21. The Bible definition of the Christian miracles, moreover, recognises the important fact that they had a complex character. Their full significance could not be apprehended by a contemplation of them from only one point of view. What they were as the "works" of Christ, working in His Father's name and in the interests of His mission, so exclusively religious and moral, could

not be all expressed by the use of a single word. Therefore three leading words are employed, each word expressing its own distinctive aspect of His works. The miracles are designated wonders, signs, and mighty works (*terata, semeia, dunameis*).

MIRACLES AS WONDERS.

22. The nature of Christ's works was such as to excite astonishment in eye-witnesses; and it is with this effect in view that the Bible calls them *wonders*. In other words, they are miracles according to the original sense of the term. But, as has already appeared, a definition of the Christian miracles would be very inadequate and vague if it took into account this subjective effect alone. For they are more than wonders. Nevertheless, viewed simply as wonders, they were of the greatest consequence; so much so, that though they could have served no other end, they might have been required in the interests of that feeling of astonishment which they created and sustained. No founder of a new religion could succeed without in some way or other appealing to the faculty of wonder. "To wonder," says Plato, "is the beginning of philosophy." Wonder is also to a large extent the parent of science. This feeling ever has been, and ever will be, a great intellectual stimulus to man. Perhaps no feeling has done more to stimulate him in his attempts to solve the mysteries of the universe and life.

23. The Christian miracles, then, presuppose this simple truth, and Christ turned it to the advantage of His cause. In His own Person and life He was the Revealer of God. Nothing was of greater consequence for the cause which He represented than that men should raise the question concerning Him, Who is this? What is He? Had these questions never been raised, Christianity never would have been founded. But the questions were raised. They are still agitating the minds of men in this remote age. And it was the miracles which first caused the questions to be asked, owing to the amazement which they pro-

duced. It is blind not to see this, or foolish not to admit it. Let it be granted that many do not require the Christian miracles to make them wonder, because they see so much in the character, and teaching, and spirit of Christ to wonder at, apart from them. Still, but for the wonder created by the miracles, when Christianity was founded, history might never have conveyed, down through the centuries, any knowledge of Christ's character and teaching to wonder at.

MIRACLES AS SIGNS.

24. Looking at another aspect of the Christian miracles, the Bible calls them *signs*. This name was applied to them in view of the ethical end in the interests of which Christ wrought them. His miracles, indeed, had more than one such end in view. They were wrought with the beneficent object of meeting some immediate want in man's earthly life; some want which appealed to His compassion, and to whose appeal He felt Himself morally free to respond. Again, many of His miracles fulfilled the purpose of illustrating the truths which He taught. But, further, they were wrought as signs; wrought, that is, to create and to encourage faith on the part of others in Himself as the Life of the World.

25. Nor was their value as signs less than their value as wonders. They were the marks or indications of something beyond themselves and different from themselves. They were signals from Christ within the natural world, to call forth man's attention and faith to realities in the spiritual world. He had come, bringing the life of God to men; come to satisfy all their higher and eternal needs. He had come to be the Life of the World in His character as the Light of the World. And His miracles stood related to the entire revelation which He sought to communicate. They were the means; the revelation itself was the end. As signs they were manifestations of His glory as the Only-begotten of the Father, full of grace and truth.

26. That which rendered the miracles necessary as signs was

the want of spiritual insight and faith in men. Hence Christ Himself valued the miracles only in so far as without them men would have remained spiritually blind and unbelieving. His principle was to bring men to receive His words and Himself, and to lead those who saw His works or heard of them from faith in the works to faith in His teaching, and in Himself as the living Truth. Consequently, to Him, that presented itself as a higher form of faith, which received Him, and believed His words, without the help of His works, than that form of faith which was so blind and weak that it could not believe unless it saw signs and wonders. Still, to originate faith, or to help it, He did not, in His wisdom, refrain from working His miracles as signs. If not without signs, then with them, if possible, He must bring men to see and believe that He was in their midst as the Light of Life sent from God to them.

MIRACLES AS POWERS.

27. According to the Bible definition, the miracles are also *powers*. The word sign (*semeion*) refers us to their final cause; the word power (*dunamis*) refers us to their efficient cause. The term power does not of itself suggest any exercise of power, or any effect from power exercised, out of the usual course of nature. It is applied to force having power to act; to force in exercise; and to that which results from the exercise of force.

28. Moreover, one of the facts most familiar to science is the fact that there are various kinds of forces at work in nature, to which the various kinds of effects produced must severally be referred. One kind of effects we refer to intellectual force; another kind to moral force; another kind to vital force; another kind to chemical force; and so on. In this respect the use of the word *power* in the Bible is rigidly scientific. According to the Bible, there are various kinds of powers or forces, and various kinds of effects corresponding to them. Nature is a manifestation of power. There is power in sin. The Spirit of Christ is power.

The gospel as a revelation is power. The cross of Christ as an atonement is power; every form of moral goodness in a Christian is power. The redemption of sinners, the kingdom of God as a thing set up on the earth, as a thing coming, and as a thing destined for consummation and eternal glory, is ascribed to power.

29. In all these connections the same word is used in the New Testament. And the same word is applied to the power which Christ exercised in the performance of His mighty works. Science shows that power is capable of being exercised in marvellously different ways; and in this respect science has the support of the Bible, as the Bible has the support of science. And so it should surprise no one to find the Bible, in connection with the Person and work of Christ, speaking of strange and marvellous exercises of power. Professedly, His mission had for its object the greatest work of God. He came to begin a work, or, at any rate, to begin the mightiest and grandest era in the history of a work, which is to end in the making of all things new.

30. Christianity presents this as its claim. And if its Founder had not inaugurated this era with some new, suitable, and striking exercises of power, some forms of modern unbelief and scepticism, which scorn or ridicule the miracles, would have easily found it convenient and self-justifiable to reject Christ because He had not vindicated His claim with signs from heaven. Does science itself not teach us, that when any new and great thing is to be done in nature, some new exercises of power must come into play? Must every effect not have an adequate cause? Has it ever been proved, or is there the least well-supported probability that it ever will be, or can be, proved, that the Christian miracles were not most necessary to render Christianity completely adequate as a cause to effect the ends which it proposes, and which nature and humanity alike are groaning to see realized? But the Bible view of miracles as powers need not be further lingered on here. Only it is important to note the fact that in Scripture they are emphasized as forces. It is mainly with regard to them as powers that science has to do.

CHAPTER III.

MIRACLES DEFINED.—NATURE.

Science rendering Definition of Miracles more easy. What is Nature: Nature difficult to define—Huxley's Definition. New Definition of Miracles. Other Definitions: Locke's Definition examined — Hume's Definition and his Argument examined—C. Hodge's Definition examined—Westcott's Definition examined. The new Definition and Science: The Definition and the Principle of Design — The Definition and God's Immanence in Nature—The Definition and Ordinary Exercises of His Power in Nature—The Definition and Extraordinary Exercises of His Power—Science bound to admit Innovations of Power in Nature.

31. The light shed by modern science upon the course of nature has done much towards rendering a precise definition of miracles possible from a physical point of view. Many of the friends of Christianity have not yet sufficiently discovered how much they are indebted to science for this result.

WHAT IS NATURE?

32. Before proceeding with a definition of miracles in relation to nature, it may be well to ask what is meant by the term, *Nature* itself. This question is not easy to answer. Our conception of nature grows with our knowledge of it. Nothing can be adequately defined without a perfect knowledge of all its aspects and relations, and of its entire history. And for that reason an adequate definition of nature is as yet quite impossible. Nature is still in course, and it may be a long way yet from its

ultimate condition. Besides, there are certain aspects and relations of nature which are still mysteries to science. For instance, science everywhere finds itself face to face with force in nature, but it cannot tell what is the essential nature of any of the forces it has discovered.

33. It is common to speak of two worlds, the natural world and the supernatural. But, then, where does the limit lie at which the one world begins and the other ends? Man belongs both to the one world and to the other. God fills nature according to Scripture, and every atom in nature is every moment sustained by Him. It is not strictly scientific to say that nature is the "*visible*" universe, or the "*material*" universe, or the "*physical*" universe. *Human* nature is a part of nature; and there is something in human nature which is not physical, not material, not visible. Freewill and self-consciousness are natural elements in man, and yet by them he is a part of that great form of existence which is called the spiritual world. Man even as a sinner belongs to the spiritual world. It is his belonging to this world that renders it possible for him to become morally guilty, and to suffer moral consequences from his transgressions. And yet his sins also imply that he is natural. In point of fact, it is impossible to give any definition of nature unless one more or less vague and provisional. The following definition is Professor Huxley's, and it is perhaps as good as any other that might be offered. "Nature," he says, "means neither more nor less than that which is, the sum-total of phenomena presented to the senses; the totality of events, past, present, and to come." This definition, as its author admits, leaves room for the possibility of such events as the Christian miracles. It is consistent with the existence of the spiritual or supernatural world. It leaves the way open for agency to pass directly out of the supernatural world into the natural world. What, then, is a miracle considered in relation to nature?

NEW DEFINITION OF MIRACLES.

34. The Christian miracles are effects from extraordinary, as distinguished from ordinary exercises, of the Personal and Divine efficiency immanent in nature; these extraordinary exercises of this efficiency being controlled by a wise and beneficent purpose.

OTHER DEFINITIONS TESTED BY THIS ONE.

35. *First*, In defining a miracle, Locke made it a condition, that as an operation it should transcend the comprehension of the spectator. This condition is not included as one of the distinctive features of miracles in the definition now offered. It is, in fact, not a distinctive feature of a miraculous occurrence at all; the truth being that there is no operation of any power in nature which is not in some respects totally beyond the comprehension of spectators, and even such spectators as have the profoundest scientific insight. What is the force of gravitation? How does it pass in its action over the distance between any two objects between which its action takes place? How by means of this force is the one body laid hold of and attracted by the other? How does the action of the will or of any other mental power produce its effect upon the nerve-force and the nerve-conditions affected by it? These are questions which science has tried in vain to answer. They concern matters which transcend our comprehension. And in like manner the operation of all the forces in nature transcends our comprehension. From this point of view, then, miracles occurring in the course of nature present no exceptional feature. Hence it only leads to confusion or misunderstanding to make it a characteristic of miracles that they must transcend our comprehension.

36. Again, Locke makes it a requisite of a miracle, that in the opinion of the spectator it should be contrary to the established course of nature. Two things are included here, neither of which

is admitted into the definition now receiving elucidation. First, Locke makes too much depend on the mere opinion of the spectator. If the spectator thinks an event is contrary to the established course of nature, it is a miracle. If he thinks otherwise, it is not a miracle. Second, he holds that no event can be regarded as a miracle, unless on the supposition that it is contrary to the established course of nature. That is to say, the notion of a miracle involves the notion of something happening inconsistent with the ordinary or fixed course of nature. In other words, a miracle is an event by which the established course of nature is violated. But science cannot admit that anything has ever happened contrary to the established course of nature. And, besides, it is not in the interest of the Christian miracles to insist on such an admission being made.

37. *Second*, This view of Locke is essentially the same as that held subsequently by many Theologians; their view being that a miracle is a violation or a transgression of the laws of nature by a particular volition of the Deity. This is the definition in connection with which Hume constructed his famous argument to disprove the credibility of the Christian miracles. And the definition, containing as it did a radical error as to the relation of miracles to natural law, gave him as a sceptic an immense advantage over those who defended them.

38. The principle of his argument was this : If two things come into competition for assent from you as a reasonable being; if in giving credence to the one you must withhold it from the other, and if the one is doubtful according to human experience while the other is certain,—then reason demands that you should give your assent to the thing that is certain, and hold as incredible the thing that is doubtful. In his argument he applied the principle in this way : Miracles are violations of the laws of nature; human testimony asks us to believe that the Christian miracles occurred; our experience convinces us that the laws of nature are never violated; it also convinces us that human testimony is often mistaken. The testimony to the occurrence of the miracles must

consequently be held as doubtful. On the other hand, it is certain from our experience that no law of nature is ever transgressed. Therefore we must give our credence to the matter that is certain, and withhold it from the one that is doubtful. That is to say, our reason, which we are bound to respect in the interests of truth, compels us to regard the occurrence of each and all of the so-called Christian miracles as utterly incredible.

39. And this is perfectly sound reasoning. But the argument falls to pieces at once when it is seen that the true definition of a miracle does not involve the conception of violence of any kind or to any extent being done to any of the laws of nature. Miracles are in reality no more justly chargeable with transgressing the laws of nature than the operations of mind are chargeable with opposition to the laws of matter; than the action of material forces is chargeable with antagonism to the laws of mind; or than the operation of any one force is contrary to the laws resulting from the action of any other force, however different in its nature. Hence in our definition of the Christian miracles no countenance is given to the notion of violence being done to nature or to natural law.

40. *Third*, Another false notion, guarded against by our definition, is that which makes a miracle consist of an event brought about in the external world by the direct agency of God, as distinguished from the action of second causes. God is the First Cause. It is possible for Him to operate in the external world. There He generally operates by means of second causes. But He may operate also, it is held, apart from second causes, and independently of them. Everything, then, that He does in the external world in this latter way is a miracle.

41. This is C. Hodge's conception of a miracle. The conception holds by a great truth, and at the same time makes a sweeping assumption. It holds by the great truth that it is possible for God immediately to exercise His volition and power in nature or the external world. But it makes the sweeping assumption, which most certainly is condemned by Scripture, that there is no

immediate action on the part of God in any of those overwhelmingly numerous events in the external world which, from custom, and perhaps from ignorance also, we refer to second causes. No man has any warrant either from the Bible or from science to exclude direct action on the part of God from any fact or event in nature. Herbert Spencer does not believe in the existence of a Personal Cause, operating immediately and everywhere in nature. In the place of the Personal God he puts an Inscrutable Power. But even he regards this Power as the Force of all the forces operating in the world of matter and the world of mind. Hence no definition of miracles claims respect which is founded on that most doubtful classification of events in the external world by which the immediate volition and action of God are admitted into a few of those events, while they are excluded from all the others.

42. *Fourth*, Westcott defines a miracle in a way which is not open to any substantial objection. (1) According to him, a miracle must be a phenomenon which cannot be explained by what we observe in the ordinary course of nature. (2) The phenomenon must be produced by the immediate working of a Personal Power. (3) Miracles are to be classified in two ways. On the one hand, there are those facts or events which are miracles in themselves, such as the Incarnation, or the raising of Lazarus from the dead; facts or events which do not arise merely from an extraordinary conjunction of ordinary causes. On the other hand, there are those events which are not in themselves miraculous, unless only in so far as they derive this character from a meeting together of ordinary circumstances in a way so strange and singular as to demand reference for their conjunction to the immediate interposition of a personal and supernatural power. To this class of miracles belong such events as the downfall of the walls of Jericho, and the immense draught of fishes secured by the disciples when they cast their nets into the water at the bidding of Christ. The various aspects of this definition are in accord with our own definition, which must now

be examined more closely. Its terms need to be looked at and tested by the requirements of science.

THE NEW DEFINITION AND SCIENCE.

43. *First*, According to the definition, the miracles happened on purpose, as means towards the accomplishment of a wise and good end. This aspect of them is not one on which science has anything to say. Whether there was indeed such an end contemplated, and whether the miracles were required and fitted to fulfil that end, must be settled on other grounds than scientific ones,—grounds hereafter to be considered.

44. *Second*, The definition embodies the idea of God's *immanence* in nature. He is present in it as an efficient cause, capable of acting in such a way as to determine the course of its phenomena. But this part of the definition will be examined when the question of God's relation to nature is considered. Meanwhile, it is enough to observe that it does not belong to science, nor has science the ability, to disprove the relation of God to nature here indicated.

45. *Third*, The definition, further, presents God as an immanent and efficient cause in nature, exercising His power in *ordinary* ways. The orderliness and constancy of nature prove that there must be orderliness and constancy in the efficiency of God, to which, ultimately, all the phenomena of nature must be referred. Moreover, as it is out of the province and power of science to deny the presence of Divine causation in nature, so likewise is it out of its province and power to deny that there is an ordinary Divine efficiency directly involved in the ordinary course of nature.

46. *Fourth*, God, as the definition also makes prominent, is free to put forth *extraordinary* exercises of His power amid the conditions of nature. In other words, it is affirmed that as there are ordinary, so there are extraordinary forms of Divine efficiency in nature; which implies, of course, that the order of nature

is such as to be capable of receiving into it *innovating* exercises of Divine volition and power. Let us look into this a little.

47. Nature is capable of receiving into its course innovating forthputtings of Divine power. Ordinary effects imply the operation of ordinary causes. And extraordinary effects suggest the operation of extraordinary causes. Some effects are so extraordinary that they are entirely or almost entirely singular. And it is a principle of science, that everything extraordinary or singular should be explained by something extraordinary or singular in the agency from which it proceeds. It is on the ground of this principle, then, that it is held that the Christian miracles, which are extraordinary or singular events, are due to extraordinary or singular exercises of Divine power.

48. And from this point of view, it would be a self-contradiction on the part of science to deny the possibility of those miracles. In point of fact, it has to admit the occurrence of events as extraordinary or singular as the Christian miracles. And, consequently, it has to admit the exercise of extraordinary or singular forms of efficiency. The beginning of nature was something extraordinary and singular. So was the origination of life on the earth. So also were the dawnings of sensation, instinct, thought, the power of self-determination, conscience. And, of course, the forms of causation from which these arose must have been correspondingly extraordinary or singular. This science is bound to admit. Whether it refers them to innovating forms of Divine efficiency or not, it cannot escape from the admission that there must have been innovating forms of efficiency of some kind or other, sufficient to account for the effects produced. Why, then, should it be considered impossible for the Christian miracles to have happened? Other events as extraordinary and singular have happened; and events which required for their production forms of efficiency not less extraordinary or singular than any of the wonders associated in Scripture with the Person and the life of Christ.

C

CHAPTER IV.

GOD'S RELATION TO NATURE.—SCIENCE.

The Question as to God's Relation to Nature necessary. Mode of Treatment. The Province of Science: God's Relation to Nature not a matter for Science to settle—Why so?—The Duty of Science as to Religious Questions. Science a Transgressor in causing Religious Doubt. Qualifications: In many instances Religion and Science deal with the same Subjects—Science helps to enlarge Conceptions of God—Science in its Discoveries is on the side of Teleology—Science tends to make Religion exact in its Knowledge—Science by its Faith in Matter is committed to Faith in Miracle.

49. Whether miracles are possible or not, depends entirely on the way in which God is related to nature. Accordingly, the question must now be asked, How is God related to nature? We may proceed at once to consider this question. It is not required that we should attempt to prove the existence of God. And already explanations have been offered of what is to be understood by the terms *miracle* and *nature*.

MODE OF TREATMENT.

50. The question of how God is related to nature is one which must be considered from different points of view; from that of science, that of religion, and that of philosophy or speculation. We shall begin with science, because of all the three it is least concerned with the question.

THE PROVINCE OF SCIENCE.

51. What has science to say regarding the relation of God to nature? It has nothing to say with authority. Science has a

province of its own; and the question now raised does not fall within this province. Every one of the special sciences deals with its own distinctive class of phenomena and questions. And one of the great secrets of modern scientific progress is the scientific habit of classifying, as far as possible, the phenomena of nature and the questions suggested by them; and the habit of requiring every distinct class of phenomena and questions to be handed over to a special and corresponding science. One of the laws of modern science is the law of scientific specialization.

52. Consequently, it is unscientific for science to undertake to answer such a question as that of God's relation to nature. And it is unscientific for any one in the interests of religion to hand over the question to science for an answer. For just as there are numerous phenomena and questions which lie outside the province of each of the special sciences, as, for instance, the phenomena and questions which lie within the province of Biology lie quite outside the province of Astronomy, so there are many phenomena and questions belonging to a province from which science in its general vocation is excluded. The question of God's relation to nature is one of these. To give an answer to this question is an undertaking which falls within the function and capacity of none of the special sciences. And it falls just as little within the function and capacity of science itself as a general method of seeking for truth. The sole region within which it is the vocation of science to seek for truth, and to affirm or deny in the settlement of questions, is the region of the experience of the senses, and of verified conclusions founded on that experience. All belonging to the region of the supernatural or spiritual world is territory for the explorations of religion and speculation alone.

53. When in the name of science, *as* science, and as distinct from speculation, attempts are made to solve questions in their nature speculative or religious, science is made responsible for a task which is not its own, and for the performance of which it

has no competent methods to use. Truth demands, and scientific habit demands, that all the different departments of truth, the more particular and the more comprehensive departments alike, shall be each investigated and determined on precisely in accordance with its own nature and requirements. Hence it would be unscientific to set before religion the task of settling questions purely scientific in their nature. Nor is there anything which scientific men better understand or more emphatically assert than this. And here they have the Bible absolutely on their side. It is a religious book. It perfectly understands its own province and vocation. And from beginning to end it never once falls into a mistake so unscientific as to attempt to enter a province or to exercise a vocation not its own, or to settle any question belonging to the vocation of science.

54. In this respect, then, science should prove itself to be as wise as religion. It should recognise the fact that religious questions belong to religion, and that speculative questions belong to speculation, just as scientific questions belong to science. And when men of science deal with questions of a religious or speculative nature, they should be careful to make it appear that they are outside the province of scientific authority. "As scientific men, we are absolutely ignorant of the subject (the nature of the Supreme Intelligence). Nor can we easily conceive information to be attainable, except by means of some trustworthy communication between the beings resident in the Unseen and ourselves. It is absolutely and utterly hopeless to expect any light on this point from *mere* scientific reasoning. Can scientific reasoning tell us what kind of life we shall find in the interior of Africa, or New Guinea, or at the North Pole, before explorers have been there? and if this be so, is it not utterly absurd to imagine that we can know anything regarding the spiritual inhabitants of the Unseen, unless we either go to them or they come to us?" (The Unseen Universe.)

SCIENCE A TRANSGRESSOR.

55. This fact, that the settlement of religious questions lies outside the vocation proper to science, is one of great practical importance. One of the effects of modern science has been to produce a vast amount of religious doubt. Arising in the first instance in the minds of certain men of science, the doubt has spread like an infection among multitudes of others, including many with little or no knowledge of the nature of the questions with which alone science has a title to deal. There is such a thing as receiving *doubt* as well as truth on authority. Modern science has spoken with the voice of authority. Its authority has been weighted with the splendour of its discoveries and with the impressiveness of its achievements. Everywhere within the civilised world immense deference to the authority of science has been developed. But, unfortunately, science has not always kept within its own proper province when it has spoken. It has undertaken in some of its representatives to speak on religious questions. It has claimed to be able to speak on such questions with authority. And by many its authority to speak on these has not been doubted. In consequence, they have accepted with deference and implicit faith all that it has said. And when its voice has been the voice of materialism, or the voice of religious scepticism, or the voice of negation or doubt as to the supernatural character of Christianity, it has not wanted many to listen to it as a gospel of truth. Hence, in the interests of Christianity it is necessary to emphasize the truth that science has no authority whatsoever to settle religious questions. Its vocation is not that of a religious guide. Therefore we do not look to science for an answer to the question, What is the relation of God to nature?

56. But what has thus been said regarding the function of science must now be qualified. It does not follow that because science cannot settle religious questions it is in conflict with

religion. The true attitude of science towards all that is true in religion, and towards Christianity in particular, is an attitude of helpfulness and harmony. Some scientific men may, indeed, be unfriendly to Christianity. But here the distinction between scientific men and science needs to be kept in view.

QUALIFICATIONS.

57. *First* qualification. In many instances science and religion have to deal with the same facts; the facts being approached and handled by science on one side, and by religion on the other. And yet in no such instance is it possible to prove the existence of the least variance or jar between the two, when each is faithful to its own vocation, and duly respects that of the other. The sickness of a child, as a fact, belongs both to the province of science and to that of religion. And the parent reconciles both science and religion in connection with this fact, when the one sends him to his physician for help, and the other sends him to God in trusting and submissive prayer. The Bible gives an account of the creation of the world from a religious point of view; and this being kept in mind, there is nothing in the account to be regarded as at variance with the physical history of the world as discovered and verified by science. It would be unscientific if religion and science did not each approach the creation of the world in its own way, and describe it from its own point of view, making use of its own terminology, and adding colour to its account from its own peculiar purpose.

58. *Second* qualification. The truths of God's existence and of His relation to nature, are truths revealed to religious faith and insight. Yet it is possible for us to have our conceptions of God and of His relation to nature enlarged and enriched by help from science. In point of fact, science has, to a very great extent, placed religion under this obligation to it, especially in more recent times. It has ranged the universe from the invisible atoms which constitute the basis of matter up to the suns and

systems of the distant spaces. It has brought to light undreamed-of marvels of forces, adaptations, and laws in nature. And every fresh discovery of science, both in the organic and the inorganic world, has supplied something new for religion to receive with gratitude, and as a help towards a worthier conception of Him who created the heavens and the earth, and who has clothed Himself with nature as with a garment.

59. *Third* qualification. Science has done much to strengthen the religious belief that nature owes its existence to a Personal and Intelligent Creator. Science is the prophet of nature. It has proved itself to be a progressive revealer of nature in its physical aspects. And few of its revelations, if any, are as impressive as those which present nature to us as a vast and complicated system of means and ends. In all directions science has unveiled the most wonderful adaptations of means to ends, of causes to effects, of organs to functions. Astronomy has a revelation of its own to give of the marvellous adaptations existing in nature. Geology has its own revelation to give also. And so with each of the other sciences which deal with nature on its physical side, with nature in its inorganic and organic aspects. The adaptation of the eye to the purposes of vision, and the adaptation of the wing to the purposes of flight through the air, are alone most impressive disclosures of the adjustment of one thing to another in nature. And yet these are but specimens of untold numbers of instances in nature which science has brought to light.

60. How, then, is nature as a system of endlessly diversified adjustments and adaptations of one thing to another to be explained? Religion explains it by the principle of design, and with reference to the intelligence of the Creator. It will not admit that the system can be adequately explained by the principle of chance, or even by the operation of blind and unconscious instinct in nature. Is the explanation offered by religion worthy of acceptation? Science is not entitled to say that it is not worthy. This is one of the problems which do not come within

the sphere of science. But science sees in all directions the adjustments and adaptations to be explained. It is ever bringing new instances of them within our knowledge. And assuming that religion is right in the explanation which it contends for, science is supplying it every day with fresh materials to add to the strength of its argument. In arguing from nature for the existence of an Intelligent Creator of the world, religion owes its first and greatest debt for help to the Bible. Its next greatest debt it owes to science. And this last portion of its debt is constantly accumulating.

61. *Fourth* qualification. The scientific method of investigation aims at exact results. It tries to reach such knowledge of the phenomena of nature as to be able to reduce them to definite laws. It seeks to come into possession of such knowledge of the history and aspects of nature as shall correspond exactly with the realities of nature. Hence the shock which modern science has given to theories and systems of thought, not constructed and reasoned out in accordance with this method. Hence religion itself, led by the example and constrained by the results of science, has been necessitated to enter upon a course of reconsideration. The Christian mind has been compelled to approach the real meaning of the Scriptures, and of the history of Christianity and of other religions, with a fresh and deepened spirit of inquiry. The consequence of this must ultimately be a large increase of fresh and deepened spiritual life among the followers of Christ. Fresh instances of contact on the part of the human spirit with the living realities of religion always mean fresh inspirations. It is one of the benefits, then, which religion owes to science, that the latter has led it, or driven it, into a path where new inspirations are to be found.

62. *Fifth* qualification. Science is bound, if it is to be consistent, to join with Christianity in holding by the possibility of miracles. In point of fact, science is bound to believe even in the actual occurrence of what must be held as miraculous. Because it believes in matter, it must believe in miracle. If matter has

existed from all eternity, without any originating cause above itself, that means a miracle in view of science. Again, if matter was created in time, and was its own cause, that means a miracle in view of science. Moreover, if matter was created by God, that still means a miracle in view of science. The existence of matter cannot be accounted for unless in some one or other of these three ways. And the adoption of any one of the explanations means faith in a miracle much more stupendous, as viewed from the standpoint of science, than any of the miracles which happened in Judea.

CHAPTER V.

GOD'S RELATION TO NATURE.—RELIGION.

This a Question for Religion. Biblical Theory defined. Biblical Theory examined: The Parts of it to be kept in view—The Wisdom of the Theory—The Theory a Proof of Divine Revelation—It implies the Possibility of Miracles—The Religion of Scripture Supernatural. Agnosticism: It has no Religious Beliefs—It has no Speculative Theory—Its Connection with Science is incidental. Positivism: Positivism defined—Its Relation to the Supernatural. Rationalism: Rationalism defined—Rationalism and Deism—Rationalism and the Miraculous—Rationalism and Reason, Scripture, Science, Speculation, Religion, Morality.

63. The question of God's relation to nature is one to which religion has a right to offer an answer with authority. We must have recourse for an answer to revelation in history, to illumination in the heart, to spiritual faith. There is a theory of God's relation to nature contained in Scripture, and which is consistent with the possibility of miracles. We shall start, therefore, with this theory as the basis of our examination.

BIBLICAL THEORY.

64. The theory of Scripture may be stated shortly under six heads.

First, God created nature (Col. i. 16).

Second, God is the upholder of nature (Col. i. 17).

Third, God transcends nature. Upon Him nature depends for its existence. But He is Himself self-existent and independent (Ps. xc. 2, cii. 25–27).

Fourth, God is immanent in nature. He dwells in it, everywhere and continually exercising His power as an efficient cause (Eph. i. 11).

Fifth, God created nature, and He continues sustaining it in existence, for purposes of holy love (Eph. i. 9-11).

Sixth, Nature is a medium of God's self-revelation to man (Rom. i. 19, 20).

BIBLICAL THEORY ESTIMATED.

65. *First,* All the elements of this theory of God's relation to nature need not be at present kept in view. What requires to be noted is, that God, according to Scripture, created nature; that He is above it; and that He is at the same time in it, as a constant source of energy and causation. There is profound wisdom in this theory, especially in the way by which it unites both the transcendence and the immanence of God in the one tie by which nature exists in dependence on Him.

66. *Second,* If Scripture had taught simply that God dwells in nature, without having any form of existence above it, this would have made Him a part of nature. The result would have been Pantheism, and miracles would have been impossible. Or, on the other hand, if Scripture had left no place in nature for the indwelling of God, but had represented Him as dwelling absolutely apart from it in His transcendence, this would have been Deism. And in this case also miracles would have been impossible. But the theory of Scripture, on the one side, exalts God above nature—exalts Him in His existence, in His nature, in His will, in His intelligence, and in His power; and yet, on the other, it brings Him into direct relation to nature, making the connection between Him and it such that everything is filled by Him; while that which is filled is different from Him. He dwells in it as the Omnipresent God; the most fundamental Being; "the Life of all that lives; the Spirit of all spirits. As He is All in all, so is all in Him."

67. *Third*, This theory of God's relation to nature is a fundamental part of the revelation contained in the Bible. Viewed in this way, it points in the direction of the conclusion that this revelation must have had a Divine origin. Perhaps science and speculation are hastening on a time, when the scriptural theory of God's relation to nature will be generally accepted as a sufficient proof, even apart from other evidences, that the revelation, of which it forms an organic part, could not be else than light from on high. Without exception, the writers of the sacred books were men unaccustomed to look at existence and things from the standpoint of speculation. They lived in an age when the methods of modern science were altogether unknown. The only kind of culture they had to help them was that of religious insight and faith. Nevertheless they, and they alone, in times which ended long ago, and which had their beginnings away far back amid the dawnings of history, perceived the relation of God to nature to be such as has been delineated. In other words, they defined that relation to be one which is in perfect accordance with all the verified conclusions of modern science, and with all the best supported speculations.

68. *Fourth*, The scriptural theory of God's relation to nature, as scarcely needs to be asserted, implies the possibility of miracles. The Bible assumes the possibility of miracles, and relates miraculous events, because it teaches that God created nature, and preserves it in existence. If God created nature, and if He upholds it in existence, then it would be the greatest possible miracle, if miracles could not happen. If the living God dwells in nature, and if in nature His will has unlimited freedom to work, it follows that there can be nothing too hard for Him to do in the interests of ends determined on by His wisdom and pursued by His holy love. This is the simple and yet profound faith of the Bible.

69. *Fifth*, One of the grand distinctions of the religion of Scripture, as it is presented there in its facts and history, is its supernatural character. Consequently, miracles are natural to it.

They are a part of its nature. It is in accordance with its nature that they should happen in time of need. The supernatural character of Christianity, however, finds no place in certain modern forms of religious scepticism and belief. And we must now go on to glance at these, and estimate their bearing on the question of God's relation to nature, and, consequently, on the question of the possibility of miracles.

AGNOSTICISM.

70. Agnosticism in its attitude towards religion is sceptical. In point of fact, it does not attempt to construct any argument to prove the impossibility of God's relation to nature as taught in Scripture. When Agnostics argue against any of the fundamental truths of Christianity, they do this on other grounds than agnostic ones. This appears at once when the nature of Agnosticism is understood. The Agnostic, *as an Agnostic*, has neither a scientific system, nor a speculative theory, nor a religious creed.

71. *First*, He can have no religious beliefs in the true sense of the term. For he does not know, and he concludes that he never can know here, any Personal God in whom he might trust, and who might be to him an object of reverence and devotion. "Agnosticism is not a religion, nor the shadow of a religion. It offers none of the rudiments or elements of religion. It is the mere disembodied spirit of a dead religion; and it has shown us that religion is not to be found anywhere within the realm of cause" (Frederick Harrison).

72. *Second*, Nor does the pure Agnostic represent any definite theory of speculation as to the origin and destiny of the universe, with man included as a part. On the contrary, the term Agnosticism means the failure of speculation. That which lies behind the phenomena of nature, it regards only as a Great Enigma, which it knows not how to solve. It calls this enigma the Unknowable. And some Agnostics dislike even the capital letter.

As speculation has seemed to them to fail so utterly, they prefer the term Unknown to the term Unknowable; since they know so little about the reality behind the phenomena of nature, that they do not even know that it cannot be known.

73. *Third*, Agnosticism is, further, not to be identified with any scientific principle or conclusion. Its connection with science is purely accidental. Some scientific men are Agnostics; and they may have become such during the course of their scientific pursuits, and in view of some of the results to which their studies have led them. But it is not their science which is responsible for their agnostic opinions. Many scientific men, as the result of their scientific studies and discoveries, have had their faith confirmed in the truths of Christianity.

74. The relation of Agnosticism to science is something like this. One of the great discoveries of science has been that of the limitations besetting it in all directions in its search for truth. The further it has gone, the more it has been made to feel that there are regions of reality into which it may not enter in quest of knowledge. This discovery, then, has been, not the cause, but the occasion of Agnosticism to certain thinkers. Science has been trusted as the only way by which knowledge can be reached. Attempts to enter those regions of truth, which lie beyond the province of science, have proved disappointing, because dependence has been placed on scientific methods and principles alone, instead of on the recognition of spiritual facts, on spiritual insight, and spiritual faith.

75. Hence Agnosticism becomes inevitable. For no kind of truth can ever be discovered by those who refuse to seek for it in its own way, and in accordance with its own requirements. The scientist seeking to understand the phenomena of the solar system, makes use of astronomical instruments and of mathematical principles. He would never commit so great a blunder as expect to find the knowledge he seeks by using, say, a microscope instead of a telescope; or by experimenting on the properties of the air instead of calculating the masses, the distances,

and the motions of the sun and the planets. And that scientist commits a blunder of the same kind, but only greater, who imagines that, if there is a Personal God above nature and in it, it would be possible to find Him apart from the existence of some degree of spiritual faith in the mind of the inquirer. For religious truth is different in its nature from scientific truth. And strict scientific principle requires that scientific truth should be sought scientifically, and that religious truth should be sought religiously.

76. Thus, then, it becomes manifest that Agnosticism is the result of an unscientific frame of mind. It in no way discredits the theory of God's relation to nature as set forth in Scripture, and consequently it has no claim to be heard as a voice against the Christian miracles. It does not deserve to be listened to as a form of religion. It does not deserve to be listened to as a speculation, for it is professedly speculation at its wits' end, and in despair. Nor does it deserve to be listened to as a genuine scientific conclusion, or as a form of scientific authority, for it owes its existence to an unscientific disregard of the conditions necessary to attain religious knowledge. Hence writers like Matthew Arnold land themselves in a contradiction, when, on the one hand, they avow themselves Agnostics, while, on the other, they dogmatize against the possibility of miracles.

POSITIVISM.

77. As a religion so called, Positivism stands related to the scriptural theory of God's relation to nature essentially in the same way as Agnosticism. The same language, up to a certain limit, is appropriate to both. Both renounce "all effort to penetrate to the reality which lies hidden behind the veil of phenomena." But Positivism differs from Agnosticism in this, that it claims to have a form of religion — "the religion of Humanity." Humanity is its substitute for God, the sum of Humanity, past, present, and future. The individual owes his

existence to Humanity. By this supreme being he is sustained and controlled. He needs no other God. His religion has no concern about an unseen God and an invisible world. He needs no supernatural Being to trust in, to love, to worship, to serve. His deity exists within the natural world, and is always visibly present with him. He needs nothing more divine, more worthy of his love and devotion, than Humanity. To be religious is to recognise the greatness and the supreme value of Humanity; to love it; to conform to all its requirements for individual and social life; to live for it.

78. Thus it will be seen that Positivism, even though its claim to be a religion were justifiable, is a religious system which excludes from its creed the idea of the supernatural. It is founded on Agnosticism. It leaves the spiritual world, "the unseen universe," out of view. So far as all that is concerned, which exists above humanity, and behind the veil of phenomena, it is agnostic. And so, like Agnosticism, it in no way lessens the value of scriptural teaching as to God's relation to nature, and as to the occurrence of miracles.

RATIONALISM DEFINED.

79. When the Rationalist carries out the principles of his system to their extreme issues, he takes up two general positions. *First*, he denies all special acts of divine interposition in the course of nature and in the concerns of men; and *second*, he holds that whatever happens in religious history must happen in ways capable of being comprehensible to the natural reason, and without having recourse to the idea of the supernatural. In point of fact, Rationalism sometimes appears in forms which do not stretch its fundamental principles to their utmost consequences. But here it is not with any particular form of the system, but with its general principles, that we have to do.

80. Rationalism must not be identified with Deism, from which it sprang. The latter banished God from nature altogether.

The Deist believed in God's transcendence in relation to nature, but denied His immanence in it. The God of Deism was too exalted to extend to nature the acts of a special providence. From the first, nature was such as to be independent of His special care and interposition. It was contrived and constructed like a self-acting machine, and made so perfect that it could be left to itself to move and take its course, determined solely by its own internal arrangements, forces, and laws. The distinctive principles of Rationalism do not go so far as this. The Rationalist may believe in the omnipresence of God in nature. But what his principles do not allow him to believe is, that God is present in nature as the Almighty, and quite unfettered in His volition and power. He may hold that God exerts influence in the world and over men. But he must so limit the exercises of His power as to leave no place among their effects for miraculous events.

81. Hence, according to the typical Rationalist, the religious history recorded in the Bible is a history which transpired without the actual occurrence of miracles. It is true that the idea of the miraculous colours the record from beginning to end. But the miraculous features must all be regarded as fictitious. They had no place among the real facts of the history as they arose. The actual history must be separated from them. And it is this actual history, sifted from the miraculous element, which is the essence of Christianity. No miracles ever occurred. There was nothing miraculous in the Person of Christ. He was a mere man, though an extraordinary religious genius and reformer, to whom the world is indebted for the high ideal of virtue which His life presented, and for the example of surpassing patience and devotion to the cause of truth and goodness shown in His death. Nor did He in reality ever work any miracles. Nor did He rise again from the dead. Nor is the new birth of the soul effected by a supernatural work of grace in the heart. Nor were any of the writers of the sacred books in any real sense miraculously inspired. Christianity in its essential character is independent of all such forms of the supernatural; and they belong to it only by

way of accident and fiction, or as the result of misunderstanding on the part of those who first propagated it.

RATIONALISM EXAMINED.

82. According to Rationalism, then, the relation of God to nature is such that it is either impossible or unnecessary that the Christian miracles should have occurred. What support has Rationalism for this position?

83. *First*, It is hard to see how it derives any support from *reason*. It seems rather to be most unreasonable to assert that either the possibility or the necessity of the Christian miracles is inconsistent with natural reason. Natural reason is limited. It is prone to err. Owing to the moral derangement of the mind in consequence of sin, reason needs revelation from without. It does not belong to reason, apart from faith, and apart from light and guidance coming to it from without, to decide what it is possible for God to do and what it is impossible for Him to do in the course of nature and history.

84. *Second*, From what has been said, it will appear that Rationalism is radically at variance with the *teaching of Scripture*. Nothing is more fundamental in the general character of scriptural teaching than the idea that miracles are both possible and necessary. While, again, the Bible throughout presents God in such a relation to nature, that the possibility of miraculous events forms an essential part of that relation.

85. *Third*, Nor does Rationalism receive any warrant from *scientific facts and principles* for holding that miracles are either unnecessary or impossible. As to the necessity for them, it would be presumption on the part of science to express any opinion either for or against. This is a question which must be solved in view of considerations of which it does not lie in the way of science, as science, to take cognizance; which at any rate cannot be recognised and interpreted apart from spiritual faith as a mental condition. Then, as to the possibility of miracles, we

have already seen that, on the one hand, it is not in the power of science to pronounce against it; while, on the other hand, science has to admit the occurrence of other events at least as extraordinary and marvellous as the Christian miracles.

86. *Fourth*, It will be seen hereafter that Rationalism is as unsupported by *speculation* as it is by science. Or rather it will be shown, from speculations based on scientific conclusions, that miracles may happen; and by a just interpretation of certain spiritual facts and conclusions it will be shown that they required to happen.

87. *Fifth*, It is easily seen that Rationalism is not supported by *religious considerations*. Religion is inseparable from the supernatural, and it is inseparable from faith. Religion presupposes the existence of faith, wonder, and reverence in the human spirit; and it presupposes qualities corresponding to these in the Divine Being, to whom the human spirit is related. These presuppositions, then, are not sufficiently recognised by Rationalism. As a system, it discourages belief in supernatural dealings on the part of God with man. It subordinates God to the order of nature, although nature has been disordered by sin. It is a discouragement to direct fellowship with God, to direct dependence on Him, to prayer, and to worship. Genuine Rationalism may produce religion in the form of "morality touched with emotion." It may seek to express itself in outward acts of worship. It may do great service to Christianity by way of expounding and enforcing its ethical truths. But if the essence of spiritual religion is a life of communion with God, the fundamental principles of Rationalism tend rather to hinder than to help it. The supreme value of Christianity as a salvation lies in its power to bring man into a life of true and abiding fellowship with God, his Father in heaven; lies in its power, that is to say, to bring man into a life of spiritual religion. And to strip Christianity of its miraculous character and history, is to shear it of its power. Hence, the interests of religion are not in favour of Rationalism, but against it.

88. *Sixth*, It is further obvious, that if Christianity with its miracles, and Christianity without them,—that is, Rationalism,—are to be judged at the bar of *morality*, the decision must be given in favour of the former. The essence of morality is moral love, rich in the powers of gratitude, self-denial, and self-sacrifice. The non-miraculous Christianity of Rationalism is Christianity deprived of its supreme power to beget such love. The supreme moral power of miraculous Christianity is the power of Divine love incarnate in the Person of Christ; Divine love revealing itself as grace, under conditions of the utmost humiliation, self-sacrifice, and suffering. And this Divine love incarnate, and so manifested, has become the mightiest power of moral causation and stimulus in human history and society.

89. Thus reason, Scripture, science, speculation, religion, and morality all join in withholding support from Rationalism in so far as it is opposed to the Christian miracles. Rationalism has nothing to rest upon but assumptions. Even nature itself, we shall find, lends no countenance to the claims against the miracles which it sets up in the name of natural reason.

CHAPTER VI.

GOD'S RELATION TO NATURE.—EVOLUTION.

Evolution does not exclude the Possibility of Miracles. Evolution a Speculation. A Study of Evolution called for in the Interest of Miracles. The Scope of Evolution. Six general Principles of Evolution. Evidence in favour of Evolution: A large Mass of Evidence seems to favour it— This Evidence does not verify it—All the Evidence is likewise in favour of Creationism. Evidence against Evolution: Evolution depends on the Principle of Continuity—It does not fulfil the Requirements of this Principle—What are Difficulties to Evolution are not such to Creationism. Miracles and Evolution as supposed verified: Evolution and Materialism, Agnosticism, and God's Immanence in Nature—Continuity defined.— As so defined it is consistent with Miracles.

90. The theory of Evolution does not necessarily imply the impossibility of miracles. Among the phenomena of nature, as understood by science, there is in reality nothing to drive the Evolutionist to the conclusion that miracles have never happened or never can happen under any circumstances. That it is impossible for miracles to happen, is a conclusion which even Professor Huxley refuses to indorse, although he is one of the most enthusiastic Evolutionists, as he is one of the most enlightened scientists of the day. It may be well, therefore, to examine in a general way the theory of Evolution, especially with the view of seeing how it really affects the question of God's relation to nature, and consequently the narrower question of the possibility of miracles.

EVOLUTION A SPECULATION.

91. At the outset it is necessary to note the fact that Evolution is only a speculation. As a theory, it exists without adequate

scientific verification. It is, indeed, one of the most stupendous and impressive speculations ever adopted by science. But it still remains, and ever may remain, a mere hypothesis; waiting in vain for that kind and for that amount of evidence required to secure for it a place among those scientific conclusions which, like the theory of gravitation, have been established beyond all reasonable doubt. It is only a theory to which science has had recourse for the explanation of certain facts observed in nature,—facts which Religion or Theology has accounted for by the theory of special acts of creation. And as the number of those facts is immense, and as the facts are presented less or more distinctly among all the various orders or groups of natural phenomena, the nature and the merits of the speculation in question require to be studied and weighed.

92. Indeed, it has become necessary to construct a defence for the possibility of the Christian miracles in view of the theory of Evolution. For doubt as to their possibility has been awakened in the minds of many who have not had it in their power to learn all that the theory implies, or all that it assumes. In the course of our examination two conclusions will be arrived at. *First*, It will be shown that the theory is unverified, and that, consequently, it cannot be regarded as opposed to the possibility of miracles. *Second*, It will be proved that on the supposition that science had verified the theory, the possibility of the Christian miracles can still be reconciled with it.

THE SCOPE OF EVOLUTION.

93. The theory of Evolution is applied now as a principle of interpretation to the entire course of phenomena throughout the visible universe. It is so applied by Herbert Spencer. The course of nature, considered as a whole, is one grand process of Evolution. It is by the theory of Evolution that the history of the solar system must be explained. The Geological history of the earth has been a history of Evolution. And still more particularly,

the out-and-out Evolutionist tells us that it is in the principles of Evolution alone that we can find the key necessary to unlock the meaning of the organic history of all living beings; of the origin and growth of mental phenomena; of the origin and growth of human society; of the origin and growth of all social and religious institutions; and of the origin and growth of languages. But the theory becomes better understood in the light of its general principles, which we shall now indicate.

GENERAL PRINCIPLES OF EVOLUTION.

94. *First*, One of the general principles of Evolution is its *opposition to the theory of special acts of creation*. When it attempts to explain the history of natural phenomena, its method is to go back to the farthest possible verge in the history of the universe before it will acknowledge itself to be in the presence of any new act of creative power. Even when the theory is worked as an instrument of interpretation by those who believe in the existence of a personal God, the effort is made to go back as far as possible—back, for instance, beyond the first appearance of man on the earth—before Creative Power is resorted to as absolutely necessary to explain the emergence of any new phenomenon in the course of nature.

95. *Second, Continuity* is another principle on which the theory of Evolution depends. This follows, of course, from the antagonism between the theory and that of Creationism. The phenomena of nature, according to the requirements of the theory, must be regarded as a chain without any missing link. The history of those phenomena is continuous, and entirely without a break. Every moment and at every stage in the history the present must be considered as the result and outcome of all past causation at work in nature, and as containing in full the cause and the promise of the entire destiny of the universe.

96. And hence it is, that it belongs to the very essence of the theory to revolt against every claim insisted on for interpositions

of Creative Power in the course of nature. The word *creation* as commonly understood does not properly find a place in the vocabulary of the theory. The theory likes the term *growth*, because it imagines that increase of size of every kind can occur without an act of creation. For the same reason it likes the term *development*, as denoting the symmetrical arrangement of parts with reference to a common centre. And for the same reason it likes the term *Evolution*, as denoting the unfolding of possibilities through a series of changes into unified systems living or dead.

97. *Third*, This brings us to another of the general principles, on which Evolution is as much dependent as it is on its principle of Continuity. This is the principle of *change*. The end of a thing is very different from its beginning; whether it be a thing that simply grows, or a thing that is developed, or a thing that is evolved. We have good reason to believe that the visible universe will not be the same when it ceases to exist as it was when it began to exist. And what is thus true with reference to the beginning and the end of the universe, is equally true with reference to the beginning and end of suns, of planets, of mountains, of crystals, of every plant, and of every animal. But there is not only this difference between the beginning and the end; there are also intermediate differences with reference both to the beginning and to the end at every stage in the history of every thing living or dead. Astronomers tell us that the sun is undergoing a process of cooling, and that implies that it can never be the same at any two successive moments of its existence. And we know for certain that no living creature is ever the same at any given moment as it will be the next.

98. That great fact, then, is the fundamental fact which the theory of Evolution sets itself to explain. It says the fact is not to be explained by the occurrence of any acts of special creation. It must all be explained on the principle of Continuity. And Continuity means, that in all the various forms of Evolution in nature, there gradually arises a series of changes. In this series of changes the law of Continuity is obeyed. The changes

of the present moment have grown out of the past one; and they are the seeds of the changes about to be. Thus changes arise from changes; thus, consequently, differences are added to differences; and thus the present of every phenomenon in nature is different from the past, and the end from the beginning.

99. We see the principle illustrated in the history of a tree from the moment that it begins to exist in the seed, till the moment when it falls into decay. Its history is that of organic changes. From first to last the number of the changes is immense. The latter end of the tree is vastly different from its original character in the germ. And yet all this difference has been effected by a gradual succession of changes, so small as to be imperceptible at the moment of their occurrence. But this principle of change on which Evolution depends is illustrated on a grander scale by the organic history of nature in general as the theory explains it. All the organic beings on the earth are divided by Zoology and Botany into kingdoms, sub-kingdoms, classes, orders, families, genera, and species. And, according to Evolution, all the different kinds of plants and animals that have existed, or still exist, had their origin in a primordial germ of life, as the tree has its origin in the seed. The overwhelming amount of difference between that first germ of life and life as now presented in all the varieties of organized beings known to science, is all to be explained independently of creative acts, and on the principle of continuous changes. Changes all but infinitely gradual, and all but infinite in number and complexity, are assumed to have arisen; and on the ground of this assumption it is concluded that organic evolution at no stage in its process required the aid of a creative hand. The human species, for example, or, say, the human brain, is nothing but a result accumulated from a series of organic changes, which started on their history with the beginning of Evolution in the primordial germ.

100. *Fourth*, It is also a general principle of the theory of Evolution that it has recourse to *long periods of time* for the solution of its problems. If the history of the phenomena, for

instance, of the organic world has consisted of a vast series of continuous changes, Evolution has no alternative but to demand for its service a period of time practically infinite. Man has been observing nature now for several thousands of years. During all those years no plant has ever been known to become an animal. Reptiles have never been known to be changed into birds. The highest apes have not presented any case where one of their number has been changed even into one of the lowest savages. No person has ever seen new organs, such as eyes, or ears, or lungs, or brains, or wings, or fins, making their first appearance in nature. All the organs existing in living creatures to-day were as perfect in them, say, six thousand years ago as they are now. But why have no such specimens of Evolution occurred during all that time? The Evolutionist answers, "The time is too short." And this answer implies that incalculable millions of years must be allowed to the theory of Evolution, if it is to explain all the changes that arose in the history of living beings before man began to observe nature.

101. *Fifth*, It is, moreover, one of the main principles of Evolution to account for the vast amount and variety of change presented, say, in the history of organic phenomena, by the *action and co-operation of a great variety of causes*. The primordial germ has proved infinitely fruitful. It was the first parent of all subsequent living beings. Every extinct and every surviving species of plants and animals were or are its offspring. It possessed the power of evolving and of being evolved into all the differences between plants and animals; into all the differences presented by all the various species, genera, and families of plants and animals; into all the differences seen in the great number and variety of organs and functions among plants and animals. How, then, have all these differences arisen? Besides requiring much time, they required many causes. Causes Astronomical, causes Geological, and causes Meteorological have been at work. Every force or agency in the inorganic world has been at work, by which it has been possible

for living beings to be affected and modified. And organic causes have co-operated with inorganic ones. The forces of need, of habit, of heredity, of natural selection, of sexual selection, have all been mighty and successful agents.

102. *Sixth*, The last principle of the theory of Evolution that requires to be specified is, that the *causes at present operating* in nature are the causes by which all that has occurred during the history of organic phenomena is to be explained. The same forces at present giving rise to changes among organic phenomena, produced all those marvellous changes, extending over untold periods of time, which Evolution undertakes to explain. Those causes, organic and inorganic, which elaborated, for example, all the different species of plants and animals up to man, are at work in nature still, and are as busy as ever; only with this advantage, that they are now receiving help in some instances from experimenting Evolutionists. Of course we do not see those causes producing results now at all such as were produced by them in Palæontological times. But we have to remember that their mode of effecting fixed and widely diversified results is infinitely slow and gradual, and that this is perfectly consistent with their powers of infinite productiveness.

Such are the salient features of the theory of Evolution. And having explained its principles, we shall now turn our attention to the evidence for and against the theory, at the same time considering how the same evidence affects the theory of special acts of creation.

EVIDENCE IN FAVOUR OF EVOLUTION.

103. The amount of evidence apparently in favour of Evolution is by no means inconsiderable. On the supposition that the theory puts us on the right track for finding out the explanation of the course of nature, it is not difficult to discover everywhere in nature phenomena which seem to agree with it. All the points of resemblance between plants and animals do so; and so do all

the points of similarity between individual plants, and between one order or group of plants and another. And what is true of plants is true of animals. In short, the phenomena of nature which appear to be in harmony with the theory of Evolution are as countless as the sand on the seashore. Hence the immense weight possessed by the theory to impress the mind and to win disciples. But the question arises, Is the theory verified by this evidence? We answer, No. It is not verified simply because it seems to have a great deal of evidence in its favour. And it is all the less verified by that evidence, owing to the circumstance that the evidence entire is capable of being reconciled with the theory of special creations.

104. *First*, The theory of Evolution is not verified by the large mass of evidence which seems to favour it. It does not follow that any theory set up to explain the course of nature, or any department of the course of nature, is true merely because it can point with utmost confidence to a large number of phenomena as agreeing with it. The force and fairness of this argument will be seen in the light of two illustrations.

105. (1.) The Optimist can furnish numberless facts from human life in support of his theory of *hope*. He can point to many phenomena which seem to indicate that there is an almighty and beneficent Will underlying all things. And everything in existence which has proved its fitness to minister to human happiness, and every form of human happiness actually experienced, encourage him to believe in the correctness of his theory. And yet, on the other hand, there is the Pessimist with as much confidence in his theory of *despair*. In support of his theory he can point to the immense amount and variety of misery beneath the load of which humanity has ever groaned. Every sorrow that has been borne, every hope that has been blasted, every tear that has been shed, every struggle to attain holiness and rest to the soul that has proved in vain,—seems to say, when looked at superficially, that "good will not be the final goal of ill," and that "man was made to mourn." In the case of each theory there

are countless facts for; but there are also countless facts against.

106. (2.) An illustration still more applicable and impressive is supplied by Astronomy. The Ptolemaic system, by which the ancients sought to explain the Astronomical aspects of the universe, was the reverse of the modern system of Copernicus. The former system assumed the earth to be stationary; and all the apparent movements of the heavenly bodies were explained with reference to the earth as the centre of the universe. The grounds on which the system rested seemed to lie beyond dispute. The existence of any kind of motion in the earth was universally unperceived. On the other hand, every one of the heavenly bodies seemed to be in motion; and on the supposition that the earth was their fixed centre, the movements observed among them appeared to be generally capable of explanation. Every sunrise and every sunset seemed in favour of the theory, and so did the nightly rising and setting of every star. Multitudes of phenomena, recurring regularly day after day and year after year, presented an aspect of harmony with the assumptions upon which the theory was constructed. Yet the theory has been proved in modern times to have been absolutely false. The system of Copernicus has completely overthrown it,—a system according to which all the movements among the heavenly bodies, that seem to have reference to the earth as the fixed centre of their occurrence, are known to be capable of actual explanation only with reference to the earth as itself a planet, and with reference to its diurnal motion on its own axis, and its annual motion in an orbit round the sun.

In like manner, then, the theory of Evolution may prove to be mistaken. And that it is destined to undergo this fortune, is all the more probable because of the argument next to be advanced.

107. *Second*, That argument is, that all the evidence which seems in favour of Evolution is equally in favour of the theory of special creations. This argument has an enlightened and honest claim to be emphasized. The theory of special acts of creation

is not contradicted by a single item of the evidence appropriated by its rival theory in its own support. If the latter theory has natural phenomena more multitudinous than the stars of heaven, all shining with apparent favour on it, the former theory can welcome and enjoy every ray of the evidence as its own. It can make itself responsible for the evidence entire. There is not the slightest necessity to ignore any amount or any aspect of the evidence, or to explain it away. Let us see how.

108. (1.) The theory of Evolution, it is to be observed, depends a great deal for support on the large extent to which similarity of type or plan prevails in the organic world. If, on the one hand, we are impressed by the infinite diversity presented to us in the organic world, we are no less impressed, on the other hand, by omnipresent likenesses. Chemistry reveals the fact that plants and animals are built up of the same classes of elements. Physiology proves that both are constructed of cells and tissues. Some plants resemble animals even in point of external configuration. The sponge is an animal, and it is so like a plant that some have referred it to the vegetable kingdom. All animals and plants alike pass through a period of growth and decay. And all of them possess powers of appropriating and assimilating food, and powers of reproduction. But what the Evolutionist lays special stress upon is likeness in type or plan. You see the same plan worked out under modifications in different species of plants. You see the same plan worked out under modifications in different species of animals. Different species of trees embody the same typical idea, and different species of birds embody the same typical idea. There are points of typical resemblance between the savage and the ape, and even between the civilised man and the ape. The same typical idea is revealed in the human hand and in the paw of a dog.

109. (2.) But, further, it is also to be observed that this prevalence of similar plan is no more in favour of the theory of Evolution than it is in favour of that of special creations. All the various resemblances to typical ideas in the organic

world may represent great typical ideas or plans that were present to the Creator's mind from all eternity, and that were brought into effect and embodied by Him in successive acts of His creative power. Watches have not been evolved from each other, though all the different kinds, from the rude one first contrived down to the most perfect one in existence, bear points of typical resemblance. Nor have steam-engines been evolved from each other. And yet there are many different kinds of them with points of typical resemblance. Nor has the breech-loading rifle been evolved from the bow and arrow of the savage, through a vast series of changes and improvements, determined partly from within and partly by environment. Yet this kind of rifle and the bow and arrow possess points of typical resemblance. In like manner there are various classes of musical instruments, and in each class the same typical idea predominates amid a great variety of modifications.

110. In all these instances, then, there is indeed a kind of evolution represented, but it is an evolution of *ideas*. And all instances in the organic world where the same type appears under modifications, are perfectly compatible with the theory of a similar evolution of ideas on the part of God; ideas adopted by Him, and allowed to control His procedure as the Creator of all things. He is the All-wise God. As the Creator, He must have had regard to order and constancy in the works of His hand. He must, consequently, have given effect in His procedure to certain typical ideas in the things which He made and established. Moreover, the evolution of His ideas in His creative procedure must have been gradual, each successive act of creation being delayed until the existing condition of things had become such as to render it appropriate and necessary. Besides, this evolution of ideas in the successive acts of the Creator did not shut out from nature the possibility of great modifications occurring there, both in the inorganic and the organic world; modifications such as science may be justified in explaining by the action of second causes.

EVIDENCE AGAINST EVOLUTION.

111. It will thus be seen that all the evidence in favour of Evolution is equally in favour of special acts of creation. But now we require to study another kind of evidence which is fatal to Evolution, while it also is quite in keeping with the requirements of the other theory. As has appeared, nature presents many facts which seem to favour Evolution. But, on the other hand, there are certain facts which are manifestly against it. The keystone in the arch of the theory of Evolution is its principle of Continuity. By this principle the theory must stand or fall. If the history of the phenomena of nature cannot be explained by the application of this principle, and if the explanations offered cannot be verified, then the theory of Evolution has no support strong enough to bear it up. If the history of natural phenomena seems to present any cases, or even but one case, of serious exception to the application of the principle, then, so far, the theory resting upon the principle is only hypothetical. Let us, then, look at the principle of Continuity as a principle of interpretation applied to nature.

112. The Evolutionist applies this principle in his attempts to explain the course of nature, and it is because he does this that he does not admit into his theory the idea of special and successive acts of creation. The question arises as to how far back the principle is to be carried in its application to the course of nature. To be consistent, the Evolutionist is bound to carry the application back to the farthest possible limit. If he must be allowed one original act of creation, he must be held limited to that by his principle. All arising after that in the course of nature must be explained by the principle, and without any further reference to acts of creation. Moreover, the explanations presented must be verified. Is, then, the principle in question able to stand this test? No. Science is not able to account for the history of natural phenomena by the principle of Continuity, understood as excluding the idea of special creation;

or, in other words, innovating exercises of Divine power. The course of nature presents gulfs which science has not been able to bridge over by applying the principle. One of those gulfs is that between dead matter and living creatures. Another is that between the plant and the animal in the organic world. Another is that between the various sub-kingdoms of plants and animals. And another is that between the highest of the lower animals and man as a self-conscious being. It is nothing but assumption on the part of science to lay the principle of continuity across these gulfs, and to conclude that this explains all, without the interposition of Creative power. Here science has little to offer but conjecture. There is nothing that it can prove by testimony or verify by experiment. It has no witness attesting that any form of life was ever evolved from dead matter, and independently of antecedent life. Nor has it any witness attesting that any form of plant life was ever evolved into any form of animal life, or that any of the lower types in the animal kingdom were evolved into higher ones. And, of course, science has never produced any of those results by way of experiment. It has done its best to originate life, but without success. And it is equally powerless to change a blackbird into a pigeon.

113. Thus, then, the course of nature at those great testing points of its history cannot be explained by the principle of Continuity. This, as a principle of complete interpretation, fails. And with this failure the theory of Evolution falls to the ground. An arch is no stronger than its keystone. Hence that with which the theory of special creation is confronted in the theory of Evolution is inadequately verified. By the former theory everything can be explained that the latter fails to account for, and everything that is consistent with the latter is equally consistent with the former.

It follows, therefore, that neither science nor speculation is entitled to demand the surrender on the part of religion of the theory of special creations to that of Evolution. The former theory has in reality no fact presented against it in nature. It goes farthest in the way of explaining all the facts to be accounted for, and none of these are a source of difficulty to it. For these reasons it has the highest claims on acceptance, especially as the other theory is so conjectural. In other words, we fall back with reasonable confidence upon the relation of God to nature as set forth in Scripture, and consequently upon the possibility of miracles which it implies. But, regarding the theory of Evolution, there is another question which it may be well to raise. Supposing the theory were to be verified by science, how would it in that case affect the question of God's relation to nature and that of the possibility of miracles?

MIRACLES AND EVOLUTION AS SUPPOSED TO BE VERIFIED.

114. *First*, The theory of Evolution does not necessarily compel any one holding it to be a Materialist. It is held by many who believe in the existence of a Personal God and Creator.

115. *Second*, Nor is there anything in the theory to drive any person holding it into Agnosticism, as some seem to suppose there is. It so happens that Herbert Spencer is both an Evolutionist and an Agnostic; and this being so in his case, and in that of others, it is apt to be supposed that the two things must have some inseparable connection. But no such connection in reality exists. What has made him an Agnostic has not been his faith in the theory of Evolution, but rather his constant habit of looking at all the phases of nature presented to him from the standpoint of science alone. He is an instance of those who have suffered from the bias produced by their too exclusively scientific modes of thinking.

116. *Third*, The theory of Evolution is capable of being explained in such a way as to make it consistent with the immanence of God in nature. To see this we must distinguish between the general principle of Evolution on the one hand, and on the other

the mode in which Evolution takes its course in nature. As to the mode of Evolution, Evolutionists are not agreed among themselves. We have seen that one of the principles of the theory is that the causes which have been at work during, for example, the history of organic Evolution, have been the same as those at present in action. Let it be granted that it has been so. And though it has been proved to the contrary, let it be assumed that the theory of Evolution accounts for the entire history of organic phenomena. Then the question arises, To what forces must the process of Evolution be referred? Is it necessary to exclude from the number of those forces the power of God as present in nature? Some Evolutionists try to explain the process in question without regard to the exercise of Divine power; while others admit the existence of this power as a constant and omnipresent efficient cause.

117. The principle of Continuity, then, strictly understood, can be reconciled with the latter view, that is, with the immanence of God in nature as an efficient cause. For what are the essential requirements of this principle? (1) It claims that nothing shall happen in nature in opposition to the course of nature. (2) It claims that every new fact coming into existence shall be accounted for by the action of a power, or a conjunction of powers, working in harmony with the entire efficiency of nature. On the assumption that Continuity is a principle adequate to the explanation of the course of nature, it can set up no higher demands than the two just named. These are its essential requirements. And it may be fearlessly asserted in the presence of modern science that they are perfectly reconcilable with the presence of a personal God in nature, and with His will operating there as the ultimate source of all causation.

118. *Fourth*, It has thus appeared that although the theory of Evolution could claim to be accepted as a scientific conclusion, still the theory is capable of an explanation consistent with the presence of Divine efficiency in nature. This, then, according to the principle of Continuity as above explained, leaves room for

original or new exercises of Divine power in nature. Such exercises of power need not be in opposition to the course of nature, and they might be in perfect harmony with every form of efficiency in nature. And this being so, a way is left open for the occurrence, not only of such events as the Christian miracles, but also for the occurrence of such events as are represented in the character of special acts of creation (Gen. i. and ii.).

CHAPTER VII.

GOD'S RELATION TO NATURE.—CONTINUITY.

Continuity explained: Importance of Continuity as a Principle--The Principle capable of many Applications—Continuity and its Relation to Power. Continuity and Miracles: Continuity and a Spiritual World—Continuity and a Personal God—Continuity and God as an Efficient Cause in Nature—Continuity and Special Acts of Creation. Special Acts of Creation defined — Special Acts of Creation consistent with Continuity. Continuity consistent with Miracles. Miracles and "The Unseen Universe:" Object of the Book — Quotations — Possibility of Miracles reconciled with Continuity—Miracles and the energy of the Unseen Universe.

CONTINUITY EXPLAINED.

119. Continuity, as one of the general principles of Evolution, has to some extent already been examined in its bearings on our subject. But the principle may be considered by itself; and its bearings on our subject are such as to render necessary a more extensive examination of it than space allowed in the previous chapter. Evolution is only one of the ways in which the principle is applied. The conception of Continuity is highly Philosophical in its nature; and it is, in fact, the one conception under which modern science attempts to unify all its knowledge. Moreover, Continuity as a scientific principle, and as rightly understood, has the highest possible claims on the respect and deference of the Christian thinker. For this principle, translated from the language of science into the language of religion, means simply that the universe in its entire history and contents has

complete and unbroken oneness in its character, arising from the One God, the One Divine Purpose, the One Divine Will, to which all stands related. Continuity is on the side of the Christian religion, and the Christian religion is on the side of Continuity. And if religion and science, in all their representatives, could but see the essential harmony of their relations to each other, on the ground of this one great principle, all variance between them would soon be at an end.

But what we have now to do is to explain more fully than has yet been done the perfect harmony existing between the principle of Continuity and what the Bible teaches us as to God's relation to nature, and the possibility of miracles.

120. The principle of Continuity may be applied in many different ways to the course and to the phenomena of nature. It may, and indeed must, be extended in its application to the spiritual world as well as to the natural world; and it must be extended to the relation between the two. There are threads of Continuity running all through the history of the universe. The stamp of Continuity is upon all organic beings. All the forces in nature operate in accordance with the principle of Continuity. The chain of Continuity links together all the successive stages and all the various aspects of human history. The history of the kingdom of God on earth has conformed to this principle. The Incarnation of the Son of God occurred at a time when conditions had been prepared through ages for the event in accordance with this principle. And in accordance with the same principle, the Divine revelation contained in the Bible entered gradually into history; as it is now, in accordance with the same principle, entering gradually and continuously into the mind and heart and life of humanity.

121. Hence it is necessary that Continuity as a principle should be distinguished from its various modes of application. And what we are now attempting is, to make it evident that the Scripture theory of God's relation to nature, including as it does the possibility of miracles, is in harmony with the *principle*.

122. Continuity implies the idea of efficient causation. That which is continuous must be *made* continuous; and this implies the operation of a cause. Continuity as a principle is essentially the embodiment of the conception of a cause or of causes operating continuously, and producing results in accordance with the efficiency from which they arise. Hence the definition of the principle of Continuity must turn on the idea of *working power*. With reference to this idea it has already been defined. The *first* requirement of Continuity is, that nothing shall be caused or happen in nature in opposition to the course of nature; and the *second* requirement is, that every new fact coming into existence in the course of nature shall be accounted for by the action of a power, or of a combination of powers, working in harmony with the entire efficiency of the universe. This principle, then, is compatible with the occurrence of the Christian miracles, and with that relation of God to nature which they presuppose. We shall now see that it is so.

CONTINUITY AND MIRACLES.

123. *First*, Continuity as a scientific principle admits of the existence of a spiritual world. With respect to this world, the only demand which it is entitled to insist upon, is that it shall exist in relation to the natural world in such a way as to involve no contradiction.

124. *Second*, Continuity is consistent with the existence of God as a Personal and spiritual Being, self-existent, and the ultimate source of power. Here all that can be required on the ground of the principle is that all things known to exist shall be capable, when fully understood, of being reconciled with His existence, nature, and will.

125. *Third*, Towards the close of the last chapter it has been shown that Continuity is, further, in perfect accordance (1) with the immanence of God in nature; (2) with the ordinary exercises of His power in nature; and (3) with the exercise of His power

in nature, in extraordinary or original ways, when occasion arises for them. For it is a fulfilment of the principle of Continuity on the part of God, if His presence in nature is consistent with it, and if all the exercises of His power are compatible with every form of energy in existence.

126. *Fourth,* We are now prepared by these steps to advance higher, and to see that Continuity is reconcilable even with special acts of creation, when the latter are understood as set forth in the Book of Genesis.

127. (1.) Let us ask, What does a special act of creation imply? Let us say that God created, for example, plant life by one creative act, and animal life by another creative act, and each of the various types of animal life by a special creative act, and man by such a creative act. What, then, does this bind us to believe? What does the Bible say we are bound to believe? Holding that God put forth those creative acts on successive occasions, as the Bible represents, we are not bound by the Bible to believe that every act of special creation was absolutely instantaneous, or that all the creative acts were absolutely alike, or that they did violence in any way to any of the orders already established in nature, or to any of the forces previously operating there. Nor are we bound to believe that no room was left by the Creator's acts for the outworkings of diversity of plan in the products of creation, that is to say, for the possibility of *Evolution under certain limitations.* Moreover, it is perfectly consistent with the nature of special creative acts, as these are described in the Bible, that the Creator in each new act should work in some way or other by means of conditions previously brought into existence by Him. Thus, then, in following the Bible in its principle of special acts of creation, we are required to believe that God is present in nature as a supreme efficient Cause, that He is perfectly free to put forth original exercises of His power, that by such exercises of His power He can bring new forms of existence into being, and that when He does this He does not consider it beneath Himself to make use, as far as may be necessary

or appropriate, of conditions which He may have previously created.

128. (2.) This definition, then, of the principle of special acts of creation as delineated in the Bible, is in absolute accordance with the scientific principle of Continuity. It would be impossible to find any two principles, whether of little or of much importance, more entirely reconcilable with each other. "We see no reason from our principles (of which one is the principle of Continuity) to question the view which asserts that man was made by a peculiar operation out of a previously existing universe" (*The Unseen Universe*).

129. *Fifth*, It now follows as a matter of course that science can have no objection to urge against the possibility of the Christian miracles on the ground of its principle of Continuity. If God's power operating in nature could effect such original results as the Bible represents in the character of special creations, and if such things could happen in accordance with that principle, then the same power must be capable of effecting, consistently with the same principle, such events as the Christian miracles. Let us go on to see how Continuity affects the question of the Christian miracles, according to the conclusions reached by the authors of "*The Unseen Universe*."

MIRACLES AND "THE UNSEEN UNIVERSE."

130. The object of this book is to reconcile the conclusions of science with the contents of the Bible as a Divine Revelation. The authors do not attempt to *demonstrate* the teachings of Christianity from the conclusions of science. What they do is to prove that the conclusions of science and the teachings of Christianity are consistent with each other. The book is an argument constructed on a physical basis for an unseen universe and a future state. From scientific conclusions the authors are led to justify, among other things, belief in a Personal God, in the creation of the visible universe by Him, and in His presence and

efficiency in nature. Continuity is one of the great principles on the lines of which their speculations are conducted. And their conclusions have all the weight that can be lent to them by ripeness of scientific knowledge and judgment regarding the physical premises from which they argue. But let us attend in particular to what the authors teach us with reference to the question we have on hand. The following are some of their own words on Continuity, on Energy, and on Miracles.

131. *First*, On Continuity : "What the principle of Continuity demands is an endless development of the conditioned. We claim it as the heritage of intelligence, that there shall be an endless vista reaching from eternity to eternity, in each link of which we shall be led only from one form of the conditioned to another."

132. *Second*, On Energy : "We are led to regard the unseen as having given birth to the present universe. We are driven to regard this Power which underlies all phenomena as Infinite and Eternal. We are led to believe that there exists now an invisible order of things intimately connected with the present, and capable of acting *energetically upon it*. The energy of the present system is to be looked upon as originally derived from the invisible universe, while the forces which gave rise to transmutations of Energy probably take their origin in the same region. We are led from these two great laws (the law of the Conservation of Mass and of Energy, and the law of Biogenesis), as well as from the law of Continuity, to regard it as at least the most probable solution that there is an Intelligent Agent operating in the universe, one of whose functions it is to develop the universe objectively considered, and also that there is an Intelligent Agent, one of whose functions it is to develop intelligence and life."

133. *Third*, On Miracles : "We can easily dispose of any scientific difficulty regarding Miracles. For if the invisible was able to produce the present universe with all its energy, it could, of course, *a fortiori*, very easily produce such transmutations of energy from the one universe into the other as would account for the events which took place in Judea. Those events are there-

fore no longer to be regarded as absolute breaks of Continuity, a thing which we have agreed to consider impossible, but only as the result of a *peculiar* action of the invisible upon the visible universe."

134. According to these conclusions, then, there is nothing whatsoever in Continuity, as a principle to which the entire course of nature conforms, to render the occurrence of miracles impossible. The principle, indeed, compels those who accept it in its full significance to hold that no break in the evolution of the visible universe can ever have taken place. And yet, on the other hand, it leaves them free to admit with consistency that the Son of God may have become human, that He may have risen from the dead, and that He may have performed all the miraculous works which He is reported to have done. But how can belief in the miracles be reconciled with the principle of Continuity so rigidly applied to the course of development in the visible universe?

135. (1.) In the *first* place, the Christian miracles are consistent with the principle of Continuity because they are not breaches of it. They are no more breaches of it than an earthquake is, or the twinkle of a star.

136. (2.) In the *second* place, they are consistent with the principle, because as occurrences they can be explained as caused by the same ultimate source of energy or efficiency as that which causes all the ordinary phenomena presented in the visible universe. Everything comes under the principle of Continuity which may be directly or indirectly referred for its existence to causation originating in the Divine Will. The Christian miracles may be referred to this ultimate source of power; and so may the unfolding or the falling of a leaf.

137. Here, then, we now find ourselves at the core of our subject. Ultimately the question of the possibility of miracles turns on the question as to the nature and range of the energy or efficiency present in the universe. The authors of "*The Unseen Universe*" tell us that they have tried to look at things with two

eyes, the eye of knowledge and the eye of faith; first with one eye, then with the other, finally with both. And they report that the present visible universe, with all the energy in it, is an evolution from the invisible universe, that there is a most intimate connection between the one universe and the other, and that the invisible order of things is capable of acting energetically upon the visible order of things. They assure us, moreover, that there is good reason to believe that there is a Divine Personal Power underlying all phenomena, and that to an Intelligent Agency must be referred the development of the visible universe and of all intelligence and life.

138. Hence we are thus conducted by way of speculation to conclude that energy is to be regarded as passing out of the unseen universe into the present visible condition of things. And the action which crosses from the unseen into the visible may sometimes be *peculiar* in its form; that is to say, it may sometimes be extraordinary or original; in which case the results would bear the character of the miraculous.

139. In effect, these conclusions, reached from arguments drawn from science, are the same as those of Scripture regarding God and His relation to nature, and His power to work mighty wonders amid the phenomena of nature, when such wonders are required in the interests of His righteousness and grace. The revelation of Scripture is, for one thing, a revelation of the entire universe as pervaded by the energy of a Personal God, the energy of an almighty Will. And, consequently, it is sublimely wise in its assumption that miracles are works not too hard for Him to perform.

140. It is to be admitted, of course, that the Christian miracles in their relation to nature surpass our comprehension. The manner in which the Divine power effected them is hidden from our view. But we ought not to object to them merely on that account. We ought rather to accuse ourselves because we realize so inadequately the mysterious and marvellous nature of the common modes of energy everywhere at work in nature. If

we wondered as much as we ought to do at what is ordinary, that in the Christian miracles which would excite our wonder, would not be so much their extraordinary character in relation to nature, as the Divine love manifested in them. One of the things happening to modern science is that it is getting its eyes opened increasingly to the marvels of the universe. And perhaps men of science will yet come to look upon that man as a marvel, who would deny the possibility of miracles while he professed to take an intelligent view of the universe.

CHAPTER VIII.

MIRACLES AND NATURAL LAW.

Natural Law not Natural Force. All Natural Laws have common Features. What is Natural Law?—(1) Natural Law depends on Natural Force—(2) Laws of Nature vary with the Forces of Nature, etc. — (3) No Natural Law is in any sense a Natural Force—(4) Natural Laws not Entities in Nature—(5) There can be no Natural Law for a Single Event. Miracles and the Definition: The Definition strictly Scientific—The Christian Miracles consistent with all the Five Elements of the Definition. What about Natural Force?

NATURAL LAW NOT NATURAL FORCE.

141. No well-enlightened scientist would now think of objecting to the possibility of miracles on the ground of *natural law*. We are indebted to science for this result. It has learnt to attach a definite and clear idea to the term natural law; and this term, taken in its strictly scientific sense, is not in the least at variance with a true conception of miracles. In order to see the perfect compatibility of miracles with the laws of nature, it is necessary to note how natural law differs from *natural force*. This distinction is of the greatest importance, and it had been well, if in the controversy between religion and science, the two things had never been confounded on the one side or the other. Unfortunately, however, the distinction between the two has often been either unperceived or ignored; and with misleading consequences, language has been used when speaking of natural law, which is quite out of place, and appropriate only when applied to natural force.

142. The laws of nature are sometimes spoken of as if they were powers, capable of acting, and of producing results. They have ascribed to them the same qualities which belong to natural forces. But this is as reckless and mischievous a blunder in the use of the language of science as has ever occurred in the use of the language of Theology. The two terms, natural law and natural force, should never be interchanged. They are not interchangeable. The character of natural law is as different from the character of natural force as that of a shadow is from that of a substance. This will appear as we attempt to answer the question, What is natural law? What are its general features?

143. The question is not about any one law of nature in particular, but about natural law as a *general conception*. One law of nature differs from another. The distinctive laws of living bodies are different from the laws of inorganic matter. The laws of motion are not the same as the laws of melody. The laws of thought differ from the laws of sensation. Every distinct class of generalized facts, and every distinct order of beings in nature, have their own distinctive laws. But there are certain features common to all the laws of nature; from the law, for instance, of mutual cohesion among the atoms of matter, up to the law of mutual attraction among the stars; from the law of motion among the planets, down to the laws of motion among the thousands of animalculæ in a drop of water. And to understand these common features of the laws of nature is to be acquainted with the general conception of natural law.

WHAT IS NATURAL LAW?

144. *First*, It is a characteristic of natural law that it is *dependent on* natural force. Without the existence of natural force, the existence of natural law would be quite impossible. If all the forces of nature were annihilated, the result would involve the complete extinction of all the laws of nature. The laws of

inorganic matter are dependent on the forces of inorganic matter, on the action of those forces, and on the effects produced by them. For the existence of every Biological law there must be Biological phenomena, and causes to which they are due. Illustrations will make this plain.

145. It is a Biological law that every living creature from the beginning to the end of its evolution passes through a period of growth and a period of decay. But upon what does this law depend? It depends (1) on the universal facts of growth and decay as belonging to the evolution of living creatures; and (2) on the forces within those living creatures and in their environment, by which the growth and the decay are caused. These forces determine the phenomena of growth and decay. And as the law in question is but an expression of the constancy with which the phenomena occur, it is manifest that it depends on the forces producing them. The law is neither the phenomena nor the forces, yet both must exist to make it possible. Again, it is in fulfilment of a natural law that each of the planets revolves in an orbit round the sun. This law is the law of orbital movement. Every planet moves in accordance with this law, and moves in accordance with it constantly. But the law has no existence apart from natural force in action. It is the action of natural force which gives rise to the general and constant phenomena, of which the law is the expression. There is, on the one hand, the force of gravitation acting on the planet as a centripetal force and tending to draw it towards the centre of the sun; and, on the other hand, the force of inertia, or the tangential force in the planet itself tending to carry it off in a straight line and at a tangent to its orbit. The action of the one force has the effect of neutralizing the action of the other; and in consequence, the resultant action produces in the planet its orbital movement. It is, then, in the case of the planet, the resultant power of the two forces now explained, which constantly impel it onward in its path around the sun. And it is to this power, acting in a similar way and producing

similar effects throughout the planetary system, that the law of orbital movement among the planets owes its existence. It is the same throughout the entire realm of natural law. Everywhere the facts of which any particular natural law is the generalized expression, are dependent on natural forces. Natural forces produce natural phenomena, and with natural phenomena, natural laws become possible.

146. *Second*, It is another general characteristic of natural law, *that different orders of natural law arise from corresponding differences among the forces of nature and their effects.* Moral laws correspond with moral forces and their effects; and the laws of the intellect correspond with intellectual powers, and the phenomena resulting from them. The laws which are the expression of Physiological forces and phenomena, are different from Psychological laws. And the laws formulated with reference to Chemical forces are different from those formulated with reference to organic forces. No feature of natural law is more general than this one, and none more apparent to the intelligent observer of nature. The action of every single force in nature produces its own phenomena. Every distinct combination of forces in action also produces its own phenomena. It is so throughout the whole of nature. And all the different natural laws framed by science are framed in accordance with corresponding differences among the phenomena to which they refer, and among the forces which are the causes of those phenomena.

147. *Third*, It will now be easy to understand as another feature of natural law, that *it is in no sense force.* No natural law is a natural force. The laws of nature never operate. They are absolutely without the power of causation. They create nothing. They evolve nothing. They contribute no kind of action to any of the operations and processes of nature. Nothing could be more unscientific than to speak of laws as efficient causes; as powers capable of doing any work in nature. They are utterly inefficient. They cause nothing. They deter-

mine nothing. Hence it follows that they are entirely without power to resist force, or to interfere in any way with causation. Neither the power of the Divine will, nor any natural force, can have resistance offered to its action by natural laws, any more than a person has resistance offered to him by a shadow when he walks across it. No single force, no combination of forces, ever has been, or ever can be, resisted in their action by natural laws. And the same is true with respect to all ordinary and all extraordinary exercises of power within the course of nature. In nature force can be resisted by force, but it cannot be resisted by law. There is nothing in law either to resist force or to be resisted by it.

148. That natural laws are entirely powerless to effect any result, is evident from the illustrations already given of the dependence of these laws on the forces of nature. But a few more illustrations may be added. It is in accordance with a natural law that plants grow towards the sun. But this law of direction in the growth of plants is not a force. It is only a result of the powers of growth on the plant and in it. The order of the blade first, then the ear, then the full corn in the ear, is another law of nature. But this order in the evolution of a plant is only an order. It is not a thing with any power of causation in it. It is caused by the forces which account for the evolution of the plant, and it is different from them. All the force which it implies is force, not in itself, but in the causes on which it depends for its existence. Or take the natural law which expresses the fact that all bodies lighter than water float when put into it, and that all bodies heavier than water sink. What causes the light body to float, and the heavy body to sink? It is not the law. Nor is the cause explained when you say the one is too light to sink, and the other too heavy to float. The light body floats because it is not strong enough in its mass to overcome the power of cohesion among the molecules of the water; and the heavy body sinks because it is strong enough to overcome that power. The question is thus entirely one of forces and their action; and

the law is only an expression of the constancy with which the forces act in nature. Or take this natural law, viz. that fluids readily change their shape. Put a quantity of water into a square vessel, and it will at once take the shape of the square vessel. And then put the same water into a round vessel, and it will immediately take the shape of the round vessel. Here also the phenomena that arise are caused not by law but by force. The molecules in water have not so firm a hold of each other as they have in a piece of stone. This places them in the former case more under the control of the force of gravitation than in the latter; and so the force of gravitation at once pulls all the molecules of the water in the vessel downwards where there is room for them to go. The change of the form of the water, consequently, has its explanation in a victory gained by one power over another, by the force of gravitation over the force of molecular attraction. And the law is merely a scientific expression of what always occurs in similar circumstances in connection with those two forces and liquids.

149. *Fourth*, Natural law, it must further be observed, is not only not a natural force, but *it is not even an entity* in nature. What are designated the laws of nature would perhaps be more properly designated if called the laws of science; for natural laws have no existence unless in the mind of the observer, and in the terms or figures which he may employ to express his ideas of what he sees in nature.

150. It is necessary to distinguish the laws of nature from those phenomena in nature with respect to which they are scientific generalizations. Let us analyse the conception common to the laws of nature to see what it involves. It involves four things quite distinct the one from the other. (1) It implies natural force. (2) It implies natural force in action. (3) It implies regular and constant orders of results following from the action of natural force. (4) It implies definite expressions in thought, or in words, or in figures, of those regular and constant orders of results. It is these expressions alone, then, that are the laws

of nature. They are entities only in scientific minds and in scientific symbols. The forces, the action of the forces, and the effects produced by those actions, are facts in nature. But natural laws are facts existing only in relation to the scientific mind, as the observer and the interpreter of nature. Hence Professor Huxley says, "A law of nature in the scientific sense is the product of a mental operation upon the facts of nature which come under our observation, and has no more existence outside the mind than colour has. Laws of nature are a mere record of our experience; upon which we base our interpretation of that which has happened, and our anticipation of that which will happen."

151. *Fifth*, One more general characteristic of natural law will now be easily understood. There can be no natural law unless with reference to instances *where nature presents a plurality and succession of the same order of phenomena*. Every singular event or phenomenon in nature excludes the possibility of natural law in relation to it so long as it stands alone. Natural law presupposes plurality, repetition, succession, similarity among the phenomena of nature. Not until events have occurred, not until they have occurred again and again and frequently, not until they present points of similarity under which they may be all classified, can there be a natural law formulated by science with reference to them. All events so singular as the Christian miracles transcend natural law. The very conception of natural law makes it a law that they should do this. So far, for example, as science knows, our planet is the only one of the solar system inhabited by living beings. This fact is a singular phenomenon of the planetary system. And hence science has never attempted to do a thing so absurd as to frame a natural law with reference to it. There is no natural law to which it can be referred, and never will be, unless it be discovered that other planets are inhabited as well. In its form, in its various motions, and in other respects, the earth presents points of resemblance to the other planets; and science has framed planetary laws as expres-

sions of these, and can explain all the planetary features of the earth with reference to them. But as to the occupation of the earth by living beings, science has to remain satisfied with it as a fact transcending all the natural laws known to it.

MIRACLES AND THE DEFINITION.

152. The definition of natural law now given is, it must be remembered, strictly scientific. And, consequently, it is one which those who have a knowledge of science, and who like to look at truth from the scientific standpoint, will readily accept. That the definition in every one of its aspects is perfectly consistent with the possibility of the Christian miracles, must be evident to every one understanding it. But this consistency may be briefly pointed out.

153. (1.) Natural law in all its orders is dependent ultimately on forces operating in nature. The Christian miracles also claim to have resulted from power working in nature.

154. (2.) All the different orders of natural law correspond with different forces, or different actions among the forces, acting as causes in the course of nature. Hence it would be out of accordance with the course of nature if new exercises of power in nature did not give rise, as in the case of the Christian miracles, to phenomena or facts, incapable of being classified under laws referring to other forces, or to other exercises of power.

155. (3.) Natural laws are themselves in no sense natural forces or causes. Nor are they even' those facts of nature which arise one by one from the action of natural forces. And so every imaginable form of opposition between the Christian miracles and natural law, in this aspect of it, is impossible, and lies out of the question. For those miracles, not being laws, should not, according to scientific demands, be expected to bear the character of inefficiency belonging to natural laws. Natural laws are neither natural phenomena produced by forces, nor are they natural forces. On the other hand, the Christian

miracles are not natural laws, but they are phenomena presented in the course of nature, as arising from power at work in nature. Moreover, like all natural phenomena, as distinguished from natural laws, and as produced by power, they possess what natural laws do not possess, the power, viz., of acting as causes in their turn. This is true of all Christ's mighty works taken as a whole; and, in particular, it is true of His Incarnation as the Son of God, and of His resurrection from the dead. For the entire miraculous history and character of Christianity forms an organic part of the power of the kingdom of God. And this power at work in human history, like every special form of energy at work in nature, is giving rise to phenomena in correspondence with its own character, that is, spiritual phenomena. And this order of phenomena, like every special order of phenomena in nature, is to be referred by the religious and scientific mind to an order of laws peculiarly its own, that is, spiritual laws. Science demands that it should be so done.

156. (4.) As natural laws, in their character as actual existences, do not exist at all unless in relation to the mind of the observer and interpreter of nature, or to the words or other symbols which he employs to register his ideas, it is obvious that nothing could be more absurd than to regard this aspect of natural law as antagonistic to the occurrence of miraculous events proceeding from forthputtings of Divine Power. How could an idea in a man's mind, or a few words or figures expressing it, hinder the Almighty from working?

157. (5.) Natural laws, owing to their essential character, can have no existence whatsoever with reference to entirely singular events appearing as phenomena in the course of nature. Such events, indeed, are the Christian miracles. But this circumstance no more brought them into discord with the laws of nature than the occupation of our planet by living beings clashes with those laws. The laws of nature cannot hinder the most singular events from arising in the course of nature. But the requirements of

natural law render it impossible for singular events to be brought under the category of natural law in any of its special groups.

158. Thus natural law as a general conception has been studied in its most rigid scientific aspects. We have turned the conception round and round on every side. We have examined and tested the possibility of the Christian miracles by it in all its lights. And we have found that this possibility is in perfect harmony with natural law in every feature of its character. Discord between the occurrence of those miracles and natural law was an absolute impossibility. Between the two there could be no more jarring than exists between the song of the lark and the silent harmonies of creation. The laws of nature offer as much freedom to extraordinary and miraculous exercises of Divine Power in the course of nature, as is offered to the bird's wing by the air, or to the journeyings of the sunbeams by the ether.

WHAT ABOUT NATURAL FORCE?

159. Natural law implies natural force. And the question arises, If miraculous power could not be resisted in its action by natural law, might it not be resisted by natural force? This is an all-important question. And in reality it is the essential and sole question demanding discussion in connection with the possibility of the Christian miracles. The question is one of perfect fairness. Science is entitled to raise it; and the Christian, in the interests of his religion, is bound to do his utmost to meet and answer it. But is it possible for him to answer it in such a way as to honour the claims which his religion has made to possess a miraculous character and history? If he can prove that the possibility of the miracles of his religion is consistent with natural force, as it is with natural law, then the entire battle is won for Christianity, as in conflict with science; and science is bound to acknowledge the victory, and to let it be carried off with honour. Moreover, we think it just as certain that Christianity will

come off victorious in the battle about natural force, as it is manifest that it has come off victorious in the battle about natural law. The grounds for this certainty will be explained farther on. Meanwhile, we must go on to prove that the occurrence of the Christian miracles was as consistent with natural laws as with natural law. These miracles actually fulfilled natural laws.

CHAPTER IX.

MIRACLES AND NATURAL LAWS.

The Question of Miracles and the Laws of Nature. Miracles and *general* Laws of Nature: (1) The Christian Miracles fulfil the Law of Efficient Causation—(2) They fulfil the Law of Final Causation—(3) They fulfil the Law of the Persistence of the Action of Force—(4) They fulfil the Law of combined Action among Forces—(5) They fulfil the Law according to which higher Forces unite in action with lower ones—(6) They fulfil the Law according to which the Action of one Force modifies that of another. Miracles and particular Groups of Natural Law: The Christian Miracles cannot be classified under such Laws—They were singular Events—Yet absolutely consistent with all such Laws.

160. We have now seen cause to believe that the possibility of the Christian miracles is in accordance with all the requirements of natural law as a general scientific conception. But there is another question of great importance which we must now meet; the question, viz., How does the possibility of those miracles stand related to natural laws? For natural law as a conception is one thing, and natural laws as facts quite another. There are *general laws* of nature, and there are *special orders* of law. And the task devolves on us now to reconcile the possibility of the Christian miracles with both.

MIRACLES AND GENERAL LAWS OF NATURE.

The Christian miracles are not only consistent with the general laws of nature, they even fulfil them. Let us prove and illustrate the truth of this statement.

161. *First*, One of the universal laws of nature is that of *efficient causes*. Every effect must have a cause, and an adequate one. We see that this, which is a fundamental principle or law of all our thinking, corresponds with all our experience of nature. Nothing that arises there is self-existent. Every phenomenon owes its existence to something beyond itself. To this law there is only one exception, viz. God. He is self-existent. All other existences owe their being to acts of causation. They are effects from the operation of adequate causes. The Christian miracles, then, fulfil this law of efficient causation. They claim to be effects from the operation of an adequate power.

162. *Second*, It is another universal law of nature that every effect has a *final cause*. Every effect comes into existence with reference to some end. No sooner does any fact in nature become understood in relation to other facts, than it throws out some hint or other as to the principle of design. The planetary system, for example, presents an immense number of phenomena all bearing the character of such apparent design as to suggest for their cause a Divine Intelligence. Again, how many instances of design seem intimated to us in the relation existing between man and the environment in which he lives! Day and night, and the various seasons of the year, minister to his necessities. And that is just another way of saying that his necessities are ministered to by the earth's motion on its axis, by its motion around the sun, by the relation of the plane of its equator to the plane of the ecliptic, and by the relation of the sun to these terrestrial conditions. The sun is his benefactor by day, and the moon by night. The earth brings forth abundantly to him. He lives by the air he breathes. Then his life is dependent on the circulation of his blood; and how marvellously contrived is the adaptation between this condition of life and the heart and other parts of the system by which it is maintained! His life also depends on a regular and continual process by means of which the venous blood forced from the heart into the lungs may be purified. And not less marvellous are the adaptations of conditions and causes by which this process is

effected; adaptations between the heart and the lungs, between the lungs and the atmosphere, between the properties of the blood and the properties of the air. Besides, to select only one example more, how exquisitely nice and mysterious are those adaptations of the various senses in man and in the lower animals to external conditions, and by means of which the sentient and intelligent being is enabled to maintain his strange relation to his environment!

163. These and all such instances as these, science, let it now be observed, is bound to accept as evidences of design. As such it is as much bound to regard them as religion is. Like religion and Theistic philosophy, it may not be bound to define the Designer as a Personal Intelligence. But it is bound at least to explain them on the ground of design as a fact in nature. It would deny its own principles and experience if it explained them otherwise. It does not admit chance among its principles as a principle of efficient causation. It denies that chance ever acts as the efficient cause of any fact in nature. It never finds anything with special adaptations for ends arising by chance in the course of nature. Besides, in all those instances, such as the system of the telegraph and the system of steam locomotion, where it has applied its knowledge of the forces and the facts of nature, it has itself acted to its credit, and with amazing success, on the principle of design. What conclusion results from this, then? The conclusion, manifestly, that science is bound in honour to itself to apply the principle or law of design for the explanation of all the adaptations presented to it among the phenomena of nature.

164. The Christian miracles then fulfil this law of design—the law of final causation. They are referred to a final as well as to an efficient cause. They occurred on purpose in the interests of a great end that was to be served by them. And Christianity asks us to regard them as necessary towards the end contemplated and as fitted to accomplish it. It asks us also to regard that end as most worthy of them. The end was the kingdom of God; the

relation of the miracles to which will in due course be examined. Meanwhile, we would assert that the Christian miracles, and especially those of the Incarnation and of the resurrection of Christ, present the most marvellous acts of obedience to the law of finality that ever have been rendered during the course of nature. It is the obedience to this law as represented by Christianity that has brought into view of men and of angels the manifold wisdom of God.

165. *Third*, A further law fulfilled by the Christian miracles is that of *the persistence of the action of natural force*. Efficient causes are forces, and universally the action of force bears the character of persistence. Natural forces act under certain conditions. The same force, or the same set of forces, might act exactly in a similar way on ever so many different occasions. On every occasion that action might take place under exactly similar conditions. These requirements being fulfilled, then, the results from the action on all the different occasions would be exactly similar to each other. And this would be one instance of obedience to the law of persistence in the action of natural force. This law is universal. So far as science knows, it receives complete fulfilment in the operation of all the forces of nature. It is because of the universal conformity to this law prevailing in nature that we are warranted to place unreserved confidence in nature, and to wait upon it for the realization of our expectations. We trust in it and we hope in it without fear of disappointment, because we know that forces absolutely alike, operating under conditions absolutely alike, will produce results absolutely alike.

166. We have to observe, then, that the Christian miracles were not a breach of this law. If it could be shown that they presented a case of exception to this one law alone, science would be compelled to regard them with the utmost incredulity. It would either have to do this, or else submit to have its confidence in nature shocked, and to distrust its great principle of Continuity, of which the persistence of the action of force is an application. But the Christian miracles are entirely reconcilable with the law

now under consideration. They fulfilled it. The Incarnation of the Son of God and all the rest of those miracles were acts of compliance with it.

167. This was how. They were strange and singular effects resulting from the action of force or of forces. But the law of the persistence of action among natural forces does not exclude, as contrary to nature, an event simply because it is strange and singular. What the law does require is this, viz., that when a strange and singular event does arise in the course of nature, it shall be explained by something correspondingly strange and singular in the cause from which it arises, or in those conditions under which the cause operates, or in both. And so it is easy to see how the Christian miracles fulfilled the law, or at least conformed to it. They resulted from extraordinary exercises of Divine Power in the course of nature, and among the action of its forces. They happened, moreover, under extraordinary conditions; and it would have been miraculous, it would have been contrary to nature, it would have been a transgression of the law we have now explained, if extraordinary effects corresponding to the extraordinary antecedents had not occurred.

168. *Fourth*, It is, again, a law of natural force, that different forces possess *the capability of combining in action.* To this law no case of exception is known to exist in nature. No force is ever presented there as isolated from all other forces, and operating out of relation with them. The principle of co-operation is one of the principles on which the entire system of energy in the universe is established, and by which every one of the natural forces in particular is regulated in its action. Everywhere forces work together, each at its own task for the common end. It is the same whether in the building up of dead matter or of living matter, whether in the building up of stars or crystals, whether in manufacturing bones or brains, whether in producing sensation or thought. Every individual phenomenon of matter and of mind, of matter dead and of matter alive, exemplifies the combination. When, for example, you see a falling star kindle up in its passage

through the atmosphere, you have before you an instance of the force of gravitation, of the force of molecular attraction, of the force of friction, of the force of heat, all united in the same object, and each contributing its own share of action towards the production of the phenomenon so soon to vanish from your sight.

169. Here, then, is another of the universal laws of nature which the Christian miracles fulfilled. It was from the action of Divine Power that those miracles arose amid the phenomena of nature. And in every one of them the law of combination as to different forces was obeyed in both of its requirements. There was neither shortcoming nor transgression. For (1) the Divine Power, as a superficial knowledge of the miracles shows, did not break the law by acting alone, and out of relation with other powers; and (2) it conformed to the law by acting in combination with other forces. In not one of the miracles was there anything done that the law forbids, or anything left undone that the law requires.

170. *Fifth*, In its action, observe once more, natural force fulfils also the law according to which *higher forces and lower forces unite in action in effecting the same result*. In nature there are various orders of forces manifested by means of their action, and which are related to each other as an ascending series. With the forces of inorganic matter the series begins. Next in order come those vital forces whose work is represented in the life of plants. Then, higher up, are those vital forces from the action of which instinct and sensation in animals arise. And, lastly, transcending all, are those mental forces of which such phenomena as thought and self-determination are products.

171. All these various orders of force, then, as revealed by their action in the production of natural phenomena, conform to a common law: the higher orders co-operate with the lower, and the lower with the higher. This is one of those natural laws which science obeys when it applies its knowledge of natural force to inventions. In every such instance it brings various forces of nature into relations with each other to produce new

results,—results which never would arise in the course of nature if left to itself. The message read off at the end of a telegraph wire means the union of higher powers with lower ones. The force of attraction holds together the molecules of the wire along which the message is conveyed. The force of electricity transmits the message. Intellectual power was needed to invent the system and to construct it. The power of intellect is required also to work the system, to compose the message transmitted, and to read it off. Then, as might be, the message acts as an exciting cause to all the forces of national revolution or of international war. The same law of union of higher forces with lower ones in action, is fulfilled in ourselves when we walk from one place to another with a deliberate purpose to discharge a duty. To explain all that happens here as one result, we must allow for the action of moral force, of intellectual force, of vital forces, of chemical force, of the force of gravitation, of the force of atomic cohesion.

172. Obedience to this law also may be claimed, it is evident, for the Christian miracles. The highest order of force in nature is capable of united action with the lowest. This science neither can nor will dispute. Nor will science be so reckless as to deny that above the highest natural force there may be a power still higher, capable of combining in action with any or with all of the other orders of force beneath it in the scale of energy. If the highest forms of human power unite in action with lower forces, then, by analogy, Divine Power may unite in action with the highest forms of power in man, and with all other forces in nature down to the inorganic ones. This is all that happened, then, in the Christian miracles. They resulted from power acting in conjunction with power, and from higher power acting in relation with lower power. When the Incarnation occurred, for example, this was Divine Power acting in relation with Biological forces. When the water was turned into wine, this was Divine Power acting in relation with Chemical forces. When the Tempest was stilled, this was Divine Power acting in relation with the

forces of Meteorology. And in all this there was actual fulfilment of the natural law now explained.

173. *Sixth*, It will be enough to reconcile the possibility of the Christian miracles with one law more. Like all the others dealt with, this law is universal : it is the law according to which *the various forces of nature modify each other in their action.* The results of every force acting in the visible universe have modifications in them, arising from the action of other forces. And what is true of single forces is true of sets of forces. It is probable that the motion of the earth around the sun has in it some degree of modification from action arising in the most distant star. The reason why the stone which we throw from us into the air changes its direction, and follows a bending course, is because the action of two forces is undergoing modification,—that of inertia and that of gravitation. The action of the mind modifies the action of the body. Hence, the nervous exhaustion which arises in consequence of mental strain. The forces at work in the body modify, on the other hand, the action of mental forces. Hence, as is now known, all forms of mental disease arise from physical derangement. So all through nature, and so among all the forces of nature.

174. As instances of the fulfilment of this law, then, every one of the Christian miracles may be explained. The modification of the action of the natural forces concerned in each of the miracles, by the action of Divine Power, is all that is required to account for what happened. And contending that such modifications arose among the action of forces, is neither more nor less than to contend for the fulfilment of a law which science must have recourse to in explaining alike all the ordinary and all the extraordinary phenomena of nature. The only question between science and religion here is the one, Whether there is a Divine Power at work in nature, by the action of which the various forces at work in nature may be modified in their action. And so far as this question is concerned, science has no right to decide.

175. Thus, then, we have seen by selecting and explaining

some of the examples of the universal laws of nature, that those laws received nothing but perfect obedience in the occurrence of the Christian miracles. And hence we are in a position now to uphold the Christian miracles as standing completely reconciled, on scientific grounds, both with the requirements of natural law and with the requirements of the universal laws of nature.

176. But one task more remains to be performed to complete the reconciliation in all directions. Besides natural law as a general conception, and the universal laws of nature, there are *particular forms* of natural law, such as those of Biology and Chemistry. Can the Christian miracles be proved to be in harmony with the particular forms of natural law also? They can.

MIRACLES AND PARTICULAR FORMS OF NATURAL LAW.

177. The only objection that can be urged against the possibility of the Christian miracles on the ground of natural law in any of its particular forms, is that they did not conform to these laws. But this objection is unscientific. They should not be expected to present instances of obedience to such laws. Besides, although they cannot be classified under any such laws, science is bound to admit their possibility; and it would be absurd for it to do otherwise.

178. It is fully admitted that those miracles transcend classification under the known laws, say, of Biology or of Chemistry. We know of no Biological law with reference to which the Incarnation of the Son of God can be explained. Neither are we able to bring the turning of the water into wine at Cana either under the category of the known laws of Chemistry, or under the category of the known laws in accordance with which wine results from an organic process. Nor have we any difficulty, or fear for the result, in admitting the same inability with respect to all the other miracles. Possibly, as some writers contend, certain of the miracles can be accounted for on the ground of special orders of natural law. All that happened in those cases where demons are

said to have been cast out, might be explicable by certain Psychological laws with which science is tolerably well acquainted. But what does it matter as to the dispute between religion and science, to conclude that such cases might be explained in that way, so long as the miracle of Christ's resurrection from the dead and other miracles are utterly incapable of being accounted for by the natural laws of any of the special sciences?

179. The true position, and the only consistent position, for an earnest believer in the Christian miracles to take up, is to hold that those miracles cannot be adequately explained from the side of nature by any of those laws of Biology, or of Chemistry, or of Psychology, etc., which science has framed in accordance with its knowledge of the phenomena of nature. This position can be defended. And science cannot refuse to admit that the grounds of the defence are scientific.

180. The Christian miracles occurred as *absolutely singular* events in the course of nature. It is as such events that they must be considered, when their possibility is tested with reference to natural law, in any of its special orders. Let us apply the test then.

181. *First*, The various orders of natural law do not receive fulfilment, unless with reference to the special orders of facts in nature, of which they are generalizations. That is to say, for example, the facts of Biology do not fulfil the laws of Astronomy. And would it not be the absurdity of all absurdities, if any man of science denied that Biological phenomena could arise in the course of nature, because these could not be explained by the laws of the solar system? The Christian miracles, then, are a class of facts of their own kind, and it would be as absurd to object to their possibility, because they cannot be explained by any special order of natural laws, as it would be to object to the possibility of vital facts, because they do not fulfil the laws of the planets.

182. *Second*, Moreover, new and singular events, which never recur, besides being consistent with special orders of natural

law, must remain above such natural laws altogether. They can have no special order of natural laws of their own, for the grand reason that they are singular. For before science can frame any natural law whatsoever, nature must furnish it with a great many events of the same kind; and must at the same time reveal bonds of order and constancy existing among them.

183. *Third*, and finally, Science has to accept the occurrence of singular events in the course of nature; events, therefore, which it is not able to explain by any of the special orders of natural law within its knowledge. Such an event was the coming into existence of the material atoms. These exist; their origination was a singular occurrence, and one by which every special order of natural laws is transcended. Another such event was the origination of life on the earth. The propagation of life, now that life does exist, can be explained by science with reference to Biological laws. But hitherto science has entirely failed, by the application of Biological laws, to explain the first advent of vital phenomena in nature. The word Biogenesis itself has been adopted by science to express its belief that the dawn of life arose from the singular exercise of a transcendent and living power. So likewise science has failed to classify under special orders of natural law the origination, in the course of nature, of sensation, intelligence, personality, self-consciousness. And yet science does not on that account deny the possibility of the existence of atoms, of life, etc. It has just as little ground, then, on which to deny the possibility of the Christian miracles, because owing to their extraordinary and singular character, they cannot be ranked under the head of any of the special orders of natural law, which have reference to special and distinct orders of natural phenomena.

CHAPTER X.

MIRACLES AND NATURAL FORCE.

The Question stated. What Natural Force is not: (1) Natural Force not Spiritual Force—(2) Natural Force not a Scientific Principle—(3) Natural Force not the Effects of its Action. What Natural Force is: (1) All Natural Force exists in Connection with Matter—(2) It is distinguished by Science from Matter—(3) Natural Force revealed as Power to Act, and as Power to receive Action—(4) Energy may be Latent as well as Active. The Conclusions and the Christian Miracles.

THE QUESTION STATED.

184. In the foregoing chapter it has been shown that the Christian miracles are consistent with natural law. They meet all the requirements of the general conception of natural law defined in terms of science. Moreover, from the general laws of nature, instances were selected and so explained as to prove that the Christian miracles can justly claim the character of having fulfilled them. Lastly, it was demonstrated that science is not entitled to object to the possibility of those miracles on the ground that they were singular events, and therefore incapable of being referred to any particular form or group of natural laws, such as the laws of Chemistry or the laws of Biology. Events as singular as the ones in question are acknowledged by science as having happened in the course of nature.

185. Having thus, then, reconciled the possibility of the Christian miracles with natural law, our next effort will be to reconcile them with *natural force.* Has science taught any-

thing regarding natural force or forces to destroy or weaken the Christian's faith in the miraculous events of the Gospel History? The answer we have to offer, and to make good, is that the teachings of science as to natural force tend rather to confirm this faith. On religious and moral grounds it can be shown that those events *required* to happen. On historical grounds it can be made evident to intelligent and unbiassed thinkers that they *did* happen. And on scientific grounds it is impossible with fairness to deny that they *could* happen. In other words, science, to be consistent with its own teachings, must admit that the possibility of the Christian miracles is in accordance with the nature and the requirements of natural force. This is what we have now to show. The entire body of the Christian miracles is compatible with all that science can teach us, and with all that it can*not* teach, with respect to natural force. What is natural force?

WHAT NATURAL FORCE IS NOT.

186. *First*, Natural force is not *spiritual force*. Spiritual forces belong to the spiritual world, and natural forces to the natural world. Any form of moral goodness, such as benevolence or integrity, and any form of sin, such as covetousness or dishonesty, are forces in the spiritual world. On the other hand, solar heat and electricity are instances of force in the natural world. At once it is evident from these instances of forces, then, that the forces belonging to the one world are totally different in their nature from those belonging to the other. They are not only not the same, they are not even analogous. In their *essential* nature, so far as known to us, solar heat is incapable of being compared as a force with any form of moral goodness as a force ; and electricity is incapable of being compared as a force with any form of sin as a force. That there must be an essential contrast between natural forces and spiritual forces is evident from the circumstance that, in the one case, the forces belong to *matter*, whereas in the other case the forces belong to *spirit*.

And between matter and spirit there is no essential identity. This essential contrast, moreover, between natural forces and spiritual forces extends to natural laws and spiritual laws. For the character of natural laws is derived from natural forces, whereas the character of spiritual laws is derived from spiritual forces. The laws of electricity, for example, are far from being the same as the laws of sin; and the laws of solar heat far from being the same as the laws of benevolence. In the spiritual world there can be no law similar to the law of gravitation, which is the scientific expression of a force acting directly as the masses concerned, and inversely as the square of the distance between them. There is no mass in God. He is a Spirit, and is, consequently, beyond the reach of the force of gravitation. Nor can His mode of acting within the spiritual world be expressed in the terms that science applies to the attraction between the earth and the sun. And what is true of God in this respect, is true of all that which, by its spiritual nature, is within the spiritual world. But we must guard against error here, by introducing three qualifications, the last of which will show that all this has a bearing of some import on the Christian miracles.

187. (1.) Many things true about forces in the natural world may also be true about forces in the spiritual world. For example, we have seen that it is a quality of natural force to be persistent in its action. On all occasions when it acts, and its actions are exactly similar, and the conditions under which it acts are exactly similar, the effects which it produces are also exactly similar. So is it in the case of sin as a force in the spiritual world. The wages of sin, the effect of sin, is spiritual death. And this effect invariably follows from sin in every instance where a mind falls under its power. This is the persistence of force in the spiritual world. And we have another manifestation of it in the power of the love of Christ. For there are certain conditions in the minds of some sinners in connection with which repentance and faith arise when the power of Christ's love reaches the heart. And in

every instance where the power of His love meets with those conditions, repentance and faith follow. In like manner forces in the spiritual world, the powers of moral goodness or the powers of sin, are capable of combining in their action, just as natural forces are capable of uniting in theirs. Hence, although we have seen that from the standpoint of science there is an essential contrast between natural forces and spiritual forces, yet there are at least superficial resemblances between them. And what is thus true of the two orders of *forces*, holds good to some extent of the *laws* belonging respectively to them. Moreover, superficial as the analogies may be in the eyes of science, in the eyes of poetry and in the eyes of religion, they may be not only real but profound. Our Lord in His teaching, and especially in His parables, has shown how beautiful, too, and how instructive they are. And no mind with any element of true poetry or of true religion in it will ever fail to experience delight in tracing and contemplating them.

188. (2.) Again, it requires to be borne in mind that there are certain *general* laws which do not belong by their own nature exclusively either to the natural world or to the spiritual world. Such are the law of efficient causes and the law of final causes. Every effect produced in both worlds by an adequate cause fulfils the one law, and every end accomplished by appropriate means and in accordance with design fulfils the other. These laws are neither natural alone nor spiritual alone, they are both.

189. (3.) Finally, we must note the circumstance, and lay stress upon it, that while there is a wide contrast essentially between the forces of the natural and the forces of the spiritual world, these two orders of forces are nevertheless so related that action and reaction can take place between them. Action passes out of the mind into the body, and it passes out of the body into the mind. By the power of Divine grace in him, a man can overcome the power of the temptation which comes to him through forces in the natural conditions of his life. By the power of temptation coming to him through these forces, a man, again, may have the

spiritual power in him overcome and weakened. That is to say, expressing the significance of the illustrations in general terms, the action of spiritual force may pass out of the spiritual world into the natural world; and the action of natural force may pass out of the natural world into the spiritual world. This is true of the forces belonging to both worlds in so far as both worlds are represented by man's condition and experience. And the point it conducts us to is this. The supernatural world is a part of the spiritual world. In this higher world the power of God, which is spiritual, is almighty and free. If, then, the action of spiritual power as it exists in man passes, as we have seen it does, into the natural world, why should the action of God's almighty power not pass out of the supernatural world into the natural world too? We are not entitled to conclude that the power of God in its action, although essentially in contrast with natural forces, is incapable of so coming into relation with those forces as to work among them, and to help them, or to overcome them. And this being so, belief in the possibility of the Christian miracles as effects resulting from Divine spiritual power acting in nature, becomes easy. This conclusion, that the action of power may cross from the spiritual world into the natural world, or rather that it must do so, was arrived at elsewhere by another route.

190. *Second*, Natural force is *not a scientific principle*. In its scientific import, a principle is something assumed as true, or something already proved to be true, and employed as an instrument of research or verification. It does not exist as an element in nature. It is not a natural force, nor the effect of a natural force. It is an element in science, and exists solely in relation to the scientific mind. It is concerned about truth in relation to nature; about truth with respect to natural forces, their actions, and their effects. Force belongs no more to the essence of scientific principles than it belongs to the essence of natural laws. There is no energy, for example, in the principle of Evolution. As a principle, Evolution is only a general idea or plan conceived by the scientific mind, and assumed as true, and in accordance

with which all the inorganic and all the organic forces of nature are supposed to have operated, while producing the course of natural phenomena. Nothing operates in nature but forces. All scientific laws, ideas, principles, belong to another category than that of force. It is impossible for them to produce a single phenomenon of nature. Therefore there can be no natural contradiction involved in the occurrence of such events as the Christian miracles considered in view of scientific principles. The only question for solution here is: Did the events occur? And if their occurrence can be established on historical or other grounds, the duty devolves on science to find out some principle for the interpretation of natural phenomena which will embrace them.

191. *Third*, It is likewise apparent that natural force itself must be distinguished from *its effects*. Indeed, nature presents few things more surprising than the differences between natural forces and the effects resulting from their action. The pain you feel is a very different thing from the spark that darts from the fire and burns your hand. It is also very different from the nerve-force that brings it into relation with your consciousness, and without which the sensation of pain would be impossible. Again, sound is a sensation existing within your consciousness. And yet—and how strange!—it must be referred, on one side at least, to nerve-force and the force of atmospheric vibrations as its causes. Vital powers are far from being the same as the food you eat; and health is far from being like bodily exercise and sleep. Yet it is in consequence of your food and of exercise and sleep acting as causes that your vital powers and health are maintained. And all this has a lesson for us. It shows that we should betray great ignorance if we concluded that the Christian miracles could not possibly happen, because as effects they are so different from the power of the Divine will by the action of which they are professedly explained.

WHAT NATURAL FORCE IS.

192. *First,* All natural force must be considered as *existing in relation to matter.* Science knows nothing of the existence of natural force apart from matter. Where force is, there matter is also. The two are coextensive in their existence. If every atom of matter were annihilated, the force of gravitation would cease to exist; and so would heat and every other form of energy in nature.

193. But it must be remembered here, that matter exists under a great variety of forms. The atoms differ. Many must have one character, and many another, and so on. Hence the difference between crystals and other stones, and the difference between one kind of crystal and another. Besides bodies solid, there are bodies liquid. The atmosphere is one kind of matter. Gases are other kinds of matter. And the ethereal substance by which space is supposed to be pervaded is still another. And all these different kinds of matter represent so many different possibilities of power. It was on the ground of this scientific truth that Paul grounded his argument for the creation of the new body of the resurrection (1 Cor. xv. 35-44). And this truth of the immense possibilities of power, suggested by the immense variety in the forms of matter presented to us, renders it unscientific to conclude that it was impossible for the Christian miracles to happen.

194. *Second,* While natural force is never known to exist apart from matter, science in its teachings *distinguishes it from matter.* The force of gravitation is not identical with the matter of the bodies which gravitate towards each other. Heat as a form of energy and as developed by friction, as when two pieces of wood are rubbed together, is not identical with the substances in which it has been raised. So with all other forms of natural force. They depend for their existence on the existence of matter. They are conditioned by matter in their action. Yet all scientific reason-

ing is based on a distinction between the forces of nature and the matter or stuff in connection with which their existence is revealed. What the nature of the relation is between force and matter, science knows not, and never may know. And this item alone of its ignorance should prove sufficient to keep it humble. In particular, it should prove sufficient to prevent it from dogmatizing against such a relation of the Divine Power, to matter, as the Christian miracles severally presuppose.

195. *Third*, Still, however, the question remains with us, What is natural force? This is a question for science to answer. All natural force is revealed to us in, and by means of, matter. All the matter in the universe exists either in the inorganic or the organic state. The various forms of force revealed in inorganic matter are physical; those revealed in organic matter are vital.

196. In all matter, whether organic or inorganic, natural force is revealed under two general aspects. On the one hand, it is revealed as power to *receive action;* and, on the other, it is revealed as power *to act*. All bodies, living or dead, present the power of being acted on, and of undergoing change; and they all present power to act and to cause change. When you hold a strong elastic band in one hand by one end and stretch it out pulling the other end with your other hand, that shows that the band has power to be acted on. And when you suddenly let one end go, the band at once springs back and makes your hand smart, and that proves that it has power to act. It is the same all through the universe of matter, living and dead. Bodies larger than the sun have power to act and to be acted on. And bodies as small as atoms have the same two forms of power. You know, too, that you act and effect changes in yourself and round about you every day; and you know that you have power to be acted on and to be changed, from the differences that circumstances and influences outside of yourself are so often causing in your thoughts and feelings.

197. This power of acting, again, which is everywhere presented

to us in nature, is also revealed under two different aspects. All the power to act in nature is not constantly in action. A vast amount of the active force in nature is capable of existing as latent energy. There is latent active power in a piece of dynamite until it is acted on by the burning fuse. There is latent active power in the corn-seed until it is cast into the soil. Then, on the other hand, all the active power in nature which is not latent is in a state of action. When you see the tide ebbing or flowing, that is a proof that the force of gravitation in the sun and the moon is busy at work on the earth. When you look into a fire burning, you see that it is a scene of great activity. The activity is that of chemical forces, that of the substance of the coal or wood and that of the oxygen of the air, rushing into union with each other. The bursting of the buds on the tree is evidence that active forces are labouring hard in them and on them. When you feel hungry some hours after your last meal, that implies that a great deal of active vital force has been expended in work during the interval.

198. Look at the Christian miracles, then, in the light of this analysis of natural force.

(1) There is a vast amount of force or power in nature to be acted on, or to receive action from other forces.

(2) There is a vast amount of force in nature to act and to cause change in that which is acted on.

(3) An immense quantity of the active force in the universe is constantly in a latent state. A great deal of this energy is either not active at all, or else it is not putting forth all its strength.

(4) All the active force which is not in a latent state is in a state of action.

199. These miracles, then, may be explained as due to outbursts of power latent in nature and coming into action. In the power of the Almighty as related to nature, there must always be an inconceivable quantity of energy latent or in reserve. Latent or reserved power in God's will is like such power in man's will;

it can be changed into a state of action. And one of the things which these miracles imply in relation to force is that some of the power in the Divine will, available for action, was translated into acts in the presence of peculiar and suitable demands and conditions.

But they imply more than reserves of power in the Divine will translated into acts. They imply also passive power, or the power of receiving action, as a quality of all those natural conditions subject to the Divine activity, which their occurrence involved. They imply latent Divine power changed into action, and passive power in nature to receive that action. What then has science to say to this? Can it in fairness object to the possibility of these miracles on this ground? Science knows two things for certain as to force. It knows that there is always a vast and unknown amount of active force, existing as latent energy in the universe. And it knows also that there is a vast and unknown amount of power always and everywhere existing in the universe ready to receive action, and to undergo change from the action of force. And knowing these two things for certain, science would display almost hopeless dogmatism if it said that such translations of latent power into acts, and such changes from those acts as the Christian miracles represent, could never have happened.

CHAPTER XI.

MIRACLES AND THE INCAPABILITIES OF NATURAL FORCE.

Introduction. Natural Force is Inscrutable: Science finds Natural Force mysterious—The Fundamental Questions of Religion and Science—The Inscrutability of Natural Force examined—Its Application to the Christian Miracles. Natural Force is Indestructible: The Law of the Conservation of Energy defined—The Bearing of the Law on the Christian Miracles. Natural Force is incapable of Self-existence: All Natural Force Relative and Dependent—Materialism disproved. The Power on which Natural Force depends: (1) This Power must be held to be Absolute, etc.—This Conclusion pointed to by Science—This View and Miracles—(2) This Power as a Person: Religion and Philosophy—This View and the Miracles—(3) What if it is uncertain whether or not the Power is Personal: Herbert Spencer—This View and Miracles.

200. Already the Christian miracles have been reconciled with natural force as distinct from spiritual force, with natural force as distinct from scientific principle, and with natural force as distinct from its effects. It has also been made evident that they are in accordance with natural force in its relations with matter; and with force as power passive and power active, as active power latent and as active power in exercise.

201. But a full definition of natural force requires to embrace its *incapabilities*. And we shall now proceed to deal with these, and to consider the Christian miracles in relation to them, one by one. There are certain incapabilities belonging to natural force as manifested under the conditions of the visible universe. What are these?

NATURAL FORCE IS INSCRUTABLE.

202. Hitherto natural force has proved itself to be incapable of being fully comprehended by scientific thought. Modern science is sufficiently well acquainted with the fact of natural force. It is able to classify a marvellously large number and variety of the effects produced in nature under the heads of the elementary forces, such as gravitation and heat. It knows that natural force acts alike within the infinitely narrow limits that exist between atom and atom, and within the infinitely wide limits that lie between the stars. The laws formulated by modern science, from the laws of astronomy down to the laws of chemistry, are a testimony to its almost miraculous discoveries of various kinds of order and constancy as pervading the universe, and arising from the modes of action among the forces there. And yet the *essential* nature of natural force, and of every one of the elementary forces of nature, is as great a mystery to the scientist as it is to the savage.

203. The fundamental question of religion is the one, What is God? And the fundamental question of science is the one, What is Force? It is the vocation of religion to answer the one question, and it is the vocation of science to answer the other. Both religion and science have tried to answer each its own question as best they could. And if it were asked, Which of the two has been the more successful? religion might humbly claim to have outstripped its fellow-seeker after truth. The Christian religion says, "God is Love; He is the Father in heaven." Christian Theology says, "God is a Spirit, infinite, eternal, and unchangeable in His Being, wisdom, power, holiness, justice, goodness, and truth." Science defines force as gravitation, atomic cohesion, chemical affinity, heat, electricity, magnetism, etc. On the one side, the definition of God leaves Him still, for religion or Theology, a Being in some respects mysterious, and with clouds and darkness round about Him. On the other side, the

definition of force leaves it still for science a great enigma. But on which side is the mystery the least, or, rather, the knowledge the greatest? May it not be replied, On the side of religion? The man who has in him the spirit of religious truth and faith comprehends and sees more of God, when he uses with intelligence the terms of the definition just given, than the best instructed scientist comprehends and sees of natural force, when he employs the terms gravitation, atomic cohesion, and all the rest. The revelation of God contained in the Gospel History, nay, even the definition of God which has been quoted from the Westminster Shorter Catechism, brings Him as a spiritual Being more within the comprehension of spiritual insight and faith, than natural force is brought within the comprehension of scientific thought by all the discoveries of this force which science has made, or by all the definitions of it which it has given. But let not men of science be upbraided on this account. Neither let science itself be depreciated. The duty devolving alike on religion and science rather is to rejoice with each other because of all the truths they do know respectively of the spiritual world and of the natural world; and to sympathize with each other in their consciousness of mystery. And, besides and withal, it is the duty of both to be thankful for the mystery, which indeed both will be, in proportion as each knows how much it is indebted to it. But we must now examine more closely the inscrutability of natural force for the sake of the object immediately in view.

204. Natural force is an all-pervading element in nature. All the discoveries of science have been discoveries of natural forces, and of their actions and effects. And all the practical applications of scientific discoveries that have been effected have been applications of natural forces. The knowledge of natural force constitutes by far the largest proportion of that knowledge which is designated scientific. The knowledge of all the physical sciences, and of all the practical sciences, is essentially knowledge concerned either about the nature of force, or the actions of force, or the effects of force. There is nothing, consequently, of which science knows so

much as it knows of force. Its knowledge of force, moreover, is so vast and so varied that it forms a splendid monument to the greatness of the powers and achievements of the human intellect. And yet in the presence of natural force science is confessedly in the presence of mysteries, whose height and depth and length and breadth it attempts in vain to comprehend. It knows natural force, and yet this force surpasses its knowledge.

205. Natural force exists in relation to atoms; but science is ignorant of the precise nature of this relation, and of the precise nature of the force involved. Again, natural force exists in relation to molecules; but here also science is as profoundly ignorant as in the former case. Once more, natural force exists in relation to the planetary and the sidereal bodies in space; but in this region of force also science is compelled to feel the limitations of its knowledge. Further, there exist mutual relations between natural force in the inorganic world and natural force in the organic world; but this is a province which science has found to be one of darkness. And the further that science has gone into the sphere of vital processes and vital forces, it has only found that the solution of one mystery has proved to be the discovery of another lying beyond. None knows so well as the expert in Biology how deep are the mysteries of life, which are but the mysteries of natural force. None knows so well as the expert in Physiology how unfathomable are the mysteries of the natural force involved in those organic cells reached by him in his last analysis.

206. What attitude, then, let us ask, is science bound to take up towards the possibility of the Christian miracles in view of the fact of the inscrutability of natural force? Nothing could possibly be more manifest than that it would involve science in utterly inexcusable presumption and dogmatism were it, in view of that fact, to assert that those miracles could never have happened in the course of nature. Science knows too much of natural force to pretend that it has succeeded in fully comprehending it in its nature and in all its possible relations. It knows that there

may be, and that there probably are, forces existing in nature which it has never yet discovered. And it is face to face with the question, What power or powers lie beyond and in immediate relation to all those forces and forms of energy ranked under the name of natural? What then? This. If any scientific man, conscious of all this, still denied the possibility of the Christian miracles, he would carry off the palm for presumption and dogmatism from those even who have made the most unwarrantable and unreasonable assertions against the conclusions of science in the name of religion or theology.

NATURAL FORCE IS INDESTRUCTIBLE.

207. It is one of the doctrines of modern science that natural force is *indestructible*. That is to say, natural force is incapable of passing into a state of non-existence without leaving behind it some form and some amount of energy to represent its full value. This is the scientific law designated *The Conservation of Energy*.

208. According to this law, the universe is full of energy. And according to the law of Continuity, which we have already considered, the energy in the universe must be infinite in point of quantity, and eternal in point of duration. Not the smallest quantity of this energy, then, can be annihilated. There are many different forms of energy in the universe; and, like so much else existing in it, these, as we shall hereafter see, are capable of undergoing change and transformation. But although energy is capable of being changed, it is not capable of being destroyed. The sum-total of energy existing in the universe ever continues an unchangeable quantity amid all its transmutations with respect to quality. All the energy at present existing as natural force in the visible universe, existed originally as energy in the invisible universe; and it will all be represented, after undergoing transformations, by its quantitative equivalent in the New Heavens and the New Earth.

209. Science, however, is not bound by its special vocation to

apply the law of the Conservation of Energy, unless within the limits of the visible creation. Within those limits the law implies the existence of absolute constancy in the amount of energy present. Much of that energy exists as latent force, and much of it exists as force in action. What is one form of force in action now, may be another form of force in action within an instant. But the same quantity of energy is upon the whole persistent.

In the visible universe there is persistence in the quantity of *matter*. Science has power to destroy life; but, as the law of Biogenesis implies, it has not power to create it. And still more is science defeated by inorganic matter. Science is absolutely without power either to destroy or to create a single atom. It can do many wonderful things with matter, as when by means of electricity it decomposes water into two perfectly different substances, oxygen and hydrogen gases; but it is powerless to bring the smallest possible particle of matter into existence, or to send one out of existence again. This, then, implies a truth with respect to natural force. If the quantity of matter is always the same, it may be inferred that the quantity of force also is always the same. For, as we have seen, force is always found where matter is. Science knows that though matter changes the forms of its existence, none of it is ever lost to nature. What is visible, like a candle, may become invisible, like a candle after it has been burnt. But if the invisible quantity of matter could be all gathered together and made visible again and weighed, it would be seen that not so much as one atom had perished. And from this and many other natural phenomena, science has good reason for the belief that the law of the Conservation of Energy expresses a great truth as to natural force; the truth, viz., that not so much energy as is needed to form a dewdrop or to transmit a sunbeam ever meets with the fate of annihilation.

210. But how does this truth bear upon the Christian miracles? It must be obvious that it is perfectly consistent with their possibility. There is nothing in the nature of those miracles, nor is there anything in the claims set up for them, which implies either

the creation of any new form of energy, or the destruction of any form of energy previously existing. These miracles represented power acting in nature, and acting in extraordinary ways. They represented also extraordinary changes amid conditions of matter and natural forces. But all this was as much in perfect unison with the fact of the Conservation of Energy as the sense of melody is with the vibrations of the air. Furthermore, the history of energy and of its conservation throughout the course of nature, as we may remind ourselves, has included the origination of other facts, undisputed by science, as singular and strange, to say the least, as the Christian miracles.

NATURAL FORCE IS INCAPABLE OF SELF-EXISTENCE.

211. In all its forms natural force is *relative, dependent, conditioned*. The scientific mind cannot conceive of it as self-existent, that is, as having no cause for its existence and persistence outside of itself. The forces of gravitation, of atomic cohesion, of chemical affinity or molecular attraction, all forms of energy, in short, known to exist in nature, must be referred by scientific thought to a cause for their existence and persistence *beyond* themselves. Science knows of no law under which to classify natural force on the assumption of its self-existence. And, what is far more, this assumption involves a contradiction of the most fundamental law upon which all scientific knowledge is built up, the law, that is, of efficient causation. But this is a contradiction of natural law which, science is compelled to hold, can never have occurred, and can nowhere exist among the phenomena of the universe. This law is the principle which underlies the entire code of natural laws from beginning to end. And if it could be proved that so much as one fact in nature existed without a cause other than itself, it would be impossible for science to have the feeling of certainty as to any of the forms of orderliness and constancy in nature, on which it so much depends and to which it owes its very existence as an instru-

ment of knowledge. Hence, as natural force is a fact in nature, science would be the chief of the transgressors of natural law if it did not regard nature as existing in constant dependence on an ulterior cause.

212. Let us, however, meanwhile assume natural force to be self-existent and unconditioned. This is the position taken up by the Materialist. His assumption means this. He believes that natural force maintains itself in existence absolutely without any support from power behind it. And he believes—must believe— either that force created itself absolutely out of nothing, or else that it never was created at all, and so must have existed from all eternity. But can natural force have existed uncreated from all eternity? Or could natural force create itself, and that from nothing? And can natural force be self-persistent, that is, can it continuously maintain itself in existence unsustained by any higher power? Any person who can believe that it can do so, and who can believe that it created itself, or that it is eternal and uncreated, believes in possibilities beyond all comparison and in every way more difficult to believe than the Christian miracles. Consequently, the last man to accuse believers in the miraculous of credulity should be the Materialist. It would be impossible for a savage to be more credulous than he is himself.

213. Our assumption that natural force is self-existent and unconditioned was made, of course, only that we might be able to see its self-contradiction. Science, on its own principles, is bound to believe that natural force depends on and is conditioned by a higher cause. But what is this cause? We must divide the answer into three parts, and reconcile each part with the possibility of miracles.

THE POWER ON WHICH NATURAL FORCE DEPENDS.

214. *First*, One thing that we are compelled to believe is that the ultimate source of power in the universe must be *absolute*, *unconditioned, independent*. All forms of the power manifested

under the conditions of nature, science necessitates us to regard as effects which must be referred for their existence, and even for their persistence, to a cause *above* themselves. The law of efficient causation, as a law of the universe, is the last law, as has just been expressed, which science, as science, can afford to give up, even in relation to but one of the infinite number of phenomena in the universe. And so, sworn by its very existence to uphold the sovereignty of this law, it says, I demand that all forms of natural force shall be regarded as effects, and as dependent; and that they shall be connected for their existence and persistence, whether by a shorter or longer chain of causation, with some self-existent and absolute Power, the uncreated and unconditioned fountainhead of all energy.

215. It is in the direction of that conclusion that science is conducting every teachable and discerning mind. And this conclusion itself, although nothing more of the character of the power were known to us, would still, for all that science could say to the contrary, leave it possible for miracles to happen. If there is an uncreated and eternal fountain of power at the head of all the energy in the universe and of all the forces in nature, and if all this energy and all these forces are constantly dependent on the fountainhead, and are, as it were, perennial outstreamings from the infinite source; who shall undertake to say in the name of science that it is impossible for miraculous events ever to arise as waves of phenomena on the streams of causation?

216. *Second*, But further, we have more to learn about this ultimate power from religion, and even from philosophy, than science has to teach us. The Christian religion not only leads us up from all the streams of energy circulating through the visible universe to their eternal uncreated source; it also teaches us that this Power is Personal and Almighty. And we are conducted to the same conclusions by the speculations contained in "*The Unseen Universe.*" How then can it be impossible on the ground of those conclusions for events like the Christian miracles to happen? If there is a Personal and an Almighty Power at the

head of all energy, and if every form of finite energy or force is every moment directly dependent on Him for its existence and its efficiency, then it follows that all the natural forces must be as dependent on His will for every one of their movements as feathers floating in the air are dependent on the breeze. And from this relation of God's power to natural force, the possibility of every miracle arises, that He might see cause to work, or to empower another to work in His name.

217. *Third*, But what if it is *uncertain that the Ultimate Power is Personal?* This is the supreme doubt in the philosophy of Herbert Spencer. His knowledge of science, and his speculations founded on his scientific knowledge, have forced the conviction on his mind that all the forces of nature, inorganic, organic, and mental alike, are dependent on a Power which is itself independent. This Power he sets up in relation to nature in place of the Christian's *Personal* God. But while he withholds from it the attribute of Personality, he ascribes to it the character of the Absolute and Omnipresent Energy. We contend, therefore, that the character with which he invests the Cause of all causes is a character in accordance with the possibility of the Christian miracles. This Cause, as he further defines it, is *Inscrutable*. It may in some sense be Personal, but it may not. He refuses to affirm personality of it. But as he affirms inscrutability, personality cannot consistently be denied. We have seen already, however, that the possibility of miracles is in accordance with the existence of an independent, absolute power, on which all other forms of power constantly depend. And much more possible must the Christian miracles have been, if this Power is the Personal God of Christianity. And Herbert Spencer's definition of the supreme Cause leaves it possible, while so many other considerations tend to make it certain, that the Christian definition of that Cause is the true one.

CHAPTER XII.

MIRACLES AND THE CAPABILITIES OF NATURAL FORCE.

Introduction. Capabilities of Natural Force: (1) Four of these restated from Chap. IX., and viewed in a new Way—Miracles in accordance with them—(2) Natural Force in Action has Power to effect Change—Miracles in accordance with this—(3) Natural Force can be overcome or resisted in its Action—Miracles in accordance with this—(4) Natural Force can be aided in its Action—Miracles in accordance with this—(5) Natural Force can be transformed—Miracles in accordance with this. The Mysteries of a Drop of Water and a tiny Flame—The Lesson they teach.

218. We now know that there are some things of which natural force is incapable. It is incapable of being fully comprehended by scientific thought, incapable of being destroyed, and incapable of existence and persistence unless in dependence on a Higher Power. And we now know also that in all these respects the possibility of the Christian miracles is entirely compatible with natural force. But our definition of natural force is not yet completed. Natural force has also wonderful *capabilities*, which still remain to be considered. We shall now, therefore, turn our attention to these, or rather to only some of them; for they are so numerous that it would take too much space to examine them all.

THE CAPABILITIES OF NATURAL FORCE.

219. Some of the capabilities of natural force have been already indicated and illustrated under the head of Natural Laws. For,

as the phenomena to which natural laws refer owe their existence to the action of natural force, it is impossible to expound natural laws without indirectly, at least, explaining natural forces at the same time. In the course of our illustration of some of those laws, we have made ourselves acquainted with four of the general capabilities of natural force. These capabilities may again be briefly noticed, not as laws, but as *facts*.

220. (1.) Natural force has the capability of *persistence in its action*. That is to say, in all cases where natural force of any kind or in any form of combination, acts in perfectly similar ways, under perfectly similar conditions, it never fails to produce perfectly similar results. Thus the movements of the moon are constantly determined by perfectly similar actions of the same forces; and so persistent is this action, that future lunar eclipses and every phase of the moon can be predicted by the Astronomer to a minute.

221. (2.) Again, it is a general capability of natural force that various forces of nature have the power of *uniting in action*. When you hold a magnet in your hand and place a needle within the range of its power, you have only to draw your hand across the table and the magnet will draw the needle after it. It is apparent that three different powers co-operate in the production of this result. There is the power you are conscious of exercising in holding the magnet and pulling it along the surface of the table. Then there is the magnetic power of the magnet by which the needle is grasped and drawn from place to place. And, finally, there is the power of atomic cohesion, without the action of which all the atoms of the magnet and of the needle would fall apart, and the magnetic relation between the two would be quite impossible.

222. (3.) Moreover, it is just as manifest that there is a general capability of *mutual action between the higher and the lower powers of nature*. In the illustration of the magnet and the needle and your experiment with them, this capability of natural

force is exemplified. Perhaps it would be too much to say that the magnetic power is higher in its nature than the power of cohesion among the atoms. But it is not too much to say that the living energy which you employ in handling the magnet is higher in its nature than both. And still higher are some powers concerned in the experiment which have not yet been noted, the powers, viz., of your mind revealed in your determining to perform the experiment, in your feeling of intellectual curiosity in watching the result, and perhaps also in the influence on your action of a desire to instruct or please some person standing by and looking on. In all this, then, there is a manifest instance of the union of higher powers with lower powers in action.

223. (4.) Then, lastly, it is a general capability of natural force that the action of one force or of any number of forces has *power to modify the action of others.* When you pull the magnet across the table, you are thereby overcoming the action of one force ; and the magnet, the force of which is quite different from that which you employ, is overcoming the same force. Before you pull the magnet, both it and the needle lie quite motionless on the table. When you pull you feel that you require to put forth some effort. That means that there is some force requiring to be overcome. It is the force of gravitation. This force keeps pulling the magnet and the needle down straight to the table as if it would pull them down through it, which it would do at once if the force of cohesion did not hold the atoms of the table together. You have to pull the magnet, then, and the magnet has to pull the needle, against the force of gravitation. And when you see the magnet move and the needle after it, that implies that the force of gravitation has been resisted in its action. It is not able to keep the magnet and the needle lying still where they were at first, because other forces are successfully acting against it.

224. It is evident, then, that the possibility of the Christian miracles is consistent with all these capabilities of natural force, *as facts in nature.* Every one of them is in perfect accord-

ance with the persistence of action among the forces of nature. And every one is capable of being regarded as an instance in which force acted in combination with force, in which higher power co-operated with lower power, and in which the action of one power was resisted by that of another.

There are, however, some other *general* capabilities of natural force which we shall now select for the purpose of argument and illustration.

225. *First*, It is a general capability of natural force, when in a state of action, *to effect change or changes in that on which it acts*. Everywhere throughout nature it is to be observed that the occurrence of change results from the action of force. Moreover, there are scientific grounds for concluding that in every instance the amount of change effected is in direct proportion to the quantity of energy expended in producing it.

226. The different quantities of solar heat distributed over different latitudes have different and corresponding values represented in the vegetation produced in those latitudes. The tidal changes produced by the attraction of the moon are much greater than those produced by the attraction of the sun; because the attraction of the former is much stronger that that of the latter, owing to its comparative nearness to the earth. More strength was required to heave up the Alps than the mountains of Britain. The stronger the force of the current, the more does it wear its banks and the farther does it carry the stones and earth that it displaces. The richer the soil is in power to produce vegetation, the more abundant is the harvest. The more muscular energy you expend within a given time, the sooner do you bring on the feeling of exhaustion.

227. All this means, then, that the action of natural force produces change, and that the greater the amount of force expended, the greater is the quantity of change effected. This is one of the universal laws of natural force, only we are now concerned with the fact rather than with the law. And what we have to notice is, that between this fact and the possibility of the New Testament

miracles there is not the least contradiction. On the other hand, the fact is highly in favour of their possibility. Every one of these miracles implied, of course, that change or changes were effected. In every instance the change was extraordinary. It implied the exercise of extraordinary power. But the miracles were professedly the effects of a Power which was more than adequate to produce them. And science is not entitled to say either that such a Power did not exist, or that it did not act adequately.

228. *Second*, It is another quality of natural force that it is capable of being *overcome or resisted in its action*. As we have seen, no natural force can be destroyed. But it must not be inferred from this that it is incapable of being counteracted. The counteraction of force by force is one of the most general phenomena of nature. Nature is, indeed, one boundless battlefield where forces are constantly meeting each other in the fight, and action is conquered by action. Nor is the fight less real or less mighty in its consequences because throughout most of the battlefield no sound of arms is heard, and the forces of nature fight in silence and in their naked strength. Moreover, wonderful as it might seem, it is the universal fight among the forces of nature, and the victories that are constantly being lost and won, that maintain the order of the visible universe and save nature from instant and utter ruin!

229. Why does the earth move in its orbit around the sun? It is because the force of gravitation is resisting the force of inertia and gaining a victory over it. And if the latter force did not suffer this defeat, millions of years ago the earth might have been in collision with some other planet or star and kindled into fire like the meteor flashing through the air. When you touch the pendulum of your clock and make it swing from side to side, you put into it a power of motion by means of which it conquers the force of gravitation every time it passes beyond the perpendicular on either side, and without which your clock would not be able to measure your time. Every hairbreadth that the plant grows taller implies that it is fighting against the force of gravitation and

winning in the conflict. When you pass your finger through a liquid, you are fighting against the power of cohesion or attraction among its molecules, and this power is defeated by you. You resist and conquer the same force when you split a piece of wood or a piece of stone, or with hammer and chisel cut a bar of iron in two. It is the same within the field of your own organic existence and life. Every moment there, forces are at war with forces; on the one side forces making for death, and on the other forces making for life. And every day there are victories and defeats on either side; and at length, after the forces making for life have done their utmost, they grow exhausted, and the forces on the other side become triumphant, and you die.

230. But this capability of natural force to resist natural force will now be distinctly seen. There is only this further requiring to be observed. Lower forces can be resisted and defeated by higher forces. This is seen, for instance, when the Lapidary takes some rough precious stone in hand, and when, by means of the powers of his will and intellect, and by means of his nervous and muscular energies, he makes use of his instruments, and cuts and grinds victoriously against the force which has been making the atoms or molecules of the stone fast in each other's embrace.

231. Here, then, as must be obvious, we have another general capability of natural force distinctly in favour of the Christian miracles. Power is capable of overcoming power. And the action of higher power is capable of overcoming the action of lower power. The Christian miracles were instances of this double quality of force. And those who have even a small amount of insight into the wonderful victories lost and won every moment among the actions of natural force, will not wonder, so far as possibility is concerned, that any of these miracles should have occurred.

232. *Third*, It is another quality of natural force that it possesses the capability of being *aided in its action*. This capability, like all the others noticed, is a general one. If nature is as if it were an immense field of battle in which forces are at

war with forces, it is also as if it were a vast *Confederation* of forces all realizing their dependence on each other and all sworn to lend each other help. The whole of nature would fall into pieces, invisible and all but infinitely small, were it not for the forces which hold the atoms and molecules together. The entire visible universe, with all the other forces in it, would instantly be plunged into confusion and ruin if the force of gravitation were annihilated. The power of solar heat is a constant minister of help to every living thing on the face of the earth. Without the aid of this power every drop of water would soon be turned into ice, and every form of living energy would die. Then think of the ministries of the inorganic forces in the soil and in the air: how constantly they are at work; how united they are in their labours; and how devoted they are to the one service of aiding the vital powers of nature. Think, too, of how the powers of your own body are evermore ministering to the powers of your mind.

233. The powers of nature, moreover, can be aided in their action by powers acting on them, or along with them, from without. Take two pieces of pure lead with one smooth surface on each. Press them together hard on their smooth surfaces, meanwhile turning one of them gently round with your hand, and you will see that in consequence the two pieces have united into one. You have been aiding one of the powers of nature. You have pressed and turned the particles of the two pieces of lead within the range of each other's attraction. And now they hold each other fast. It is the same kind of help that the blacksmith gives to the same force when he welds two pieces of iron into one by making them red-hot and smiting them together with his hammer on the anvil. And in the same way you would aid the force of gravitation in the sun if you had power and exercised the power to bring all the planets to rest in their orbits. Immediately the force of gravitation would cause them all to gravitate towards the centre of the sun with a mighty rush, and each of them in its turn would be swallowed up as in a lake of fire.

234. Thus, then, we have gained a clear perception of another great capability of natural force, viz. that of its being aided in its action. And with this we have gained another point of view from which to reconcile the miracles of Christ's Person and history with the forces of nature. Science knows of mighty and most wonderful things being done by force overcoming force; and it knows of things as mighty and wonderful being done by force aiding force. And in so far as any of those miracles in their occurrence implied the aiding of natural forces by the action of Divine power, science may be challenged to prove, even by analogies, that it was impossible for the aid to be given on the one side or to be received on the other.

235. *Fourth*, We must limit our argument to one illustration more. Natural force presents the capability of *being transformed*. In some respects this is the most wonderful and mysterious capability of all. And it adds greatly to the proof, already reached, in favour of the contention that the mighty works of Christ's Person and history could happen.

236. The fact that natural force is capable of undergoing transmutation is the fact to which expression is given in the great scientific law of *the Transformation of Energy*. The law of Continuity, the law of the Conservation of Energy, and the law of the Transformation of Energy represent some of the most splendid achievements of science. In other chapters the possibility of the Christian miracles has been proved to be in conformity with the first and the second of these laws. And now it will be easy to prove its conformity also with the third.

237. Science, as has been pointed out, makes a distinction between natural force and the matter or stuff with which it is always associated in nature. This stuff consists of atoms, and, so far as science knows, not one of those atoms ever changes its character. It is probable that different kinds of atoms have existed from the first. But there is no evidence that any of the orders of those ultimate elements of matter ever undergo transformation. There are many different kinds of matter; but

Chemistry explains them all as various combinations of the ultimate particles of the substance of the visible universe.

238. Natural force, however, is otherwise known to science. It is the most changeable thing in nature; and it is the cause of all the changes of which nature is everywhere and evermore the scene. The character, the forms, and the amount of the transmutations of natural force are represented by the changes presented in the phenomena of nature. The course of nature has been a process of action among its forces and of transformations of force into force. Testimony to such transformations is borne by every inch of rock in the crust of the earth and by every particle of dust on its surface. Long ago, it might be millions of years, solar energy was transformed and stored up in the vast coal-beds of the world, where it has lain ever since as latent energy. Look at your fire burning. You learn another lesson from it on the transformation of energy. The heat emitted by it reports to you the fact that the latent energy of the coal, which has slept throughout such vast ages, has been aroused from its slumber as transmuted energy in the form of heat. And it is the oxygen of the air which has disturbed its repose.

239. Let us take other lessons from a steam-engine at work and from the machinery which it is driving. Here is presented to us a wonderful instance of natural and mechanical power and effect. Where does the heat come from that we feel in the axles of the wheels when we touch them? This is the power of mechanical friction changed into the energy of heat. But where does all the mechanical power come from that is represented by the mechanical movements which we see in process? This question takes us to the power of steam. It is the power of steam transformed that appears in all the movements that we note. And so, in its turn, the power of steam is a transformation of the latent energy of the coal burning in the furnace; just as this latent energy in the coal is, as we have seen, transformed solar energy, perhaps millions of years old.

240. But science has far greater wonders than these to show us.

It can show us chemical force turned into electricity, and electricity turned into magnetism. And it can take the force in a magnet and change it into electricity, chemical action, heat, and light. And still more marvellous are other transformations of natural forces with which science is familiar. How different is a living body from the chemical properties of inorganic matter! One of the great differences between the two is one in point of energy. There is not one spark of vital energy in all the inorganic world. When we pass out of this world into the world of living plants and living animals, we meet with forces altogether new. Where did these vital forces come from? They are so many different kinds of energy, drawn originally from the inorganic world, and transformed in the process. So science teaches us. And we know also that every plant and every animal that die and are turned to dust and ashes, present to us instances of vital forces being transformed into dead ones.

241. Why, then, with this fact of the marvellous transformations of natural force in view, should any person ever think of doubting or denying the possibility of the Christian miracles on scientific grounds? As science has grown in acquaintance with the stupendous capabilities of the forces of nature, its eyes have been opened to behold with astonishment that transmutations among those forces is one of them, and that transitions are constantly occurring from side to side, even between the higher and the lower forms of energy. And the law of the Transformation of Energy is both the stamp which science has put on this mysterious fact of nature, and one of the laurels of triumph which science has wreathed in its own crown.

242. Transformation of Energy! This is what happened at the instant when the Son of God, through His mother, entered into His incarnate relation to humanity. This is what happened when He rose again from he dead. This is what happened when He healed the sick, cleansed lepers, made the lame to walk, opened the eyes of the blind, or did any other of His mighty deeds. The Christian miracles speak to us of Divine

Power working in nature. This Divine energy was transformed through its extraordinary action, and through its relation to the natural forces concerned, into the Incarnation, and into all the other miracles. We wonder as we contemplate these transmutations of energy from the standpoint of nature. But we are not unbelieving. And science does much to support our faith. For we distinguish between science itself and those who speak in its name against the Christian miracles, without understanding it, and without hearkening to the voice of its testimony.

243. In the interests of these miracles, then, we appeal to science, on the ground of its law of the Transformation of Energy. And here is its intelligent and honest answer. It says, "Wonder, indeed, at the transmutations of power involved in these miracles. But if you have valid historical evidence in favour of these occurrences, along with religious and moral reasons, let your wonder be mixed with faith. I know of transformations of energy as wonderful as these. And everywhere I look, and every moment I please to look, I can see these wonders transpiring before my eyes. I have my miracles as well as the religion for which you claim them. And though religion could claim them by the thousand, I could claim them by the tens of thousands. I have discovered this visible universe to be so full of the transformations of power, and of transformations of power that are so constantly in process, that I have been compelled to attach to them the significance of one of my greatest laws."

244. And science has sufficient occasion so to speak. Looking at the Christian miracles in relation to the known forces and processes of nature, neither religion nor science can explain how one of them occurred. The Incarnation of the Son of God, for instance, and His resurrection from the dead, are mysteries to both. But science is equally unable to explain the precise nature of the process involved in any of the transformations, which it knows to occur as a fact, among the forces of nature.

245. Before a drop of water and a tiny flame science stands

in the presence of mysteries as unfathomable to it as are all the miracles of the New Testament. (1) The drop of water has power to extinguish the flame. (2) The water can be decomposed into hydrogen and oxygen gases in the proportion of two to one. (3) Oxygen, one of the elements of the fire-extinguisher, is the agent which nature employs to make combustibles burn. (4) Hydrogen, the other element of the fire-extinguisher, itself is capable of burning with a blue flame. (5) Yet hydrogen will give no support to the flame of any other combustible. (6) When hydrogen burns, it unites with the oxygen of the air and forms water. These are scientific facts, and their relations to one another and the transformations of energy which they involve, bring science into the presence of mysteries as profound as the Christian miracles.

246. Let us then sit at the feet of the drop of water and of the tiny spark as their humble disciples, and lay to heart the lesson they have to teach us. It is this. They say, Hearken! Earnest and intelligent faith in that which is miraculous or mysterious is the last thing in this universe of wonders that should be made an occasion of variance or reproach between the friends of science and the friends of religion.

CHAPTER XIII.

THE INCARNATION POSSIBLE.—SCIENCE.

The Incarnation as a Characteristic of Christianity. The Incarnation as a striking Fact. Science has a Title to inquire into the Possibility of the Incarnation. The Incarnation and Biology: How Biology has to do with it — The Biological Question — Why Biology must admit the Possibility of the Incarnation. The Incarnation and the Biologist: An Explanation—(1) The Biologist as a Creationist and the Incarnation—(2) The Biologist as an Evolutionist and the Incarnation. The Incarnation and the Theory of Organic Evolution in general: General Statement—Groups of salient Facts—Does the Process of Evolution continue? If so, In what direction? The Incarnation fulfils the requirements indicated.

247. The Incarnation is the supreme characteristic of Christianity. It is this as a fact, and as a medium for the historical revelation of God and of eternal life; and it is this also, because it was required to make Christianity possible as a redeeming power. Christianity, as Matthew Arnold is pleased to acknowledge, is the greatest and happiest stroke ever yet made for human perfection. But he fails to understand that Christianity never could have made this stroke, but for the power that it derived from the Incarnation. He evidently thinks that he has thrown just discredit on the Incarnation, when he has asserted that "the fundamental thing for Christians is not the Incarnation, but the imitation of Christ." There is, however, in this connection an all-important question to be considered, viz. Whether, without the Incarnation, Christians ever could have had Christ to imitate.

248. The Incarnation is the most startling fact within the

knowledge of man, when considered from a *religious* point of view. It is so, whether we look up from the fact to God, or down from the fact to man; whether we think of it as a revelation of the possibility on the part of God to come down into union with man, or of the possibility on the part of man to be taken up into union with God. It is, moreover, one of the most startling facts within the knowledge of man, when viewed from the standpoint of *science*. But here observe a difference is made: we do not say *the* most startling, but *one* of the most startling. For, while there is indeed no fact known so startling to religious thought as that of the Incarnation, there are many other facts fitted to startle scientific thought as much, if not even more. Scientific men, for example, must hold either that God did create the material atoms, or that He did not create them; and in either case they believe in something more startling from their point of view than the Incarnation. Again, the Biologist must accept either the law of Biogenesis or the law of Abiogenesis; he must either believe, that is to say, that no form of life can come into existence apart from antecedent life, or believe that life is capable of arising from inorganic conditions by spontaneous generation; and here also belief in either alternative suggests something which should startle science more than what is suggested by the occurrence of the Incarnation.

249. In its relation to nature the Incarnation involves questions of possibility as to natural conditions and forces which science has a right to examine; as much so, as it has to inquire into the origin of atoms, or of life, or of species, or of intelligence, or of the appearance of a sixth finger on a human hand. But here it requires to be borne in mind that there is a distinction between science and the sciences. Science is entitled to raise the question of the possibility of the Incarnation. But *all* the sciences are *not* entitled to raise it. This title belongs to Science in only one of its branches, viz. that of Biology. Whether the Incarnation was possible, is a question neither for Astronomy, nor for Geology, nor for Chemistry, nor for any other of the

special sciences: it is a question for Biology alone. And, consequently, it matters not in what special department of science any man may happen to be an expert, he is entirely incompetent to express an opinion against the possibility of the Incarnation, till he has become to some extent a Biologist, and has in particular made himself acquainted with all the Biological information that bears less or more directly on the question.

THE INCARNATION AND BIOLOGY.

250. The question of the *pre-existence* of Christ as the Son of God is one for religion, not for Biology. All Biological questions with reference to Christ must begin and end with Him as an individual human being. And even as a human individual He presents questions for Biology only on the organic side of His existence and life. All the mental phenomena apparent in man belong to the science of Psychology. And it is only those phenomena apparent in him as a member of the animal kingdom, and as at the head of that kingdom, that are subjects proper for Biological investigation.

251. According to the teaching of Christianity, then, Christ had only *one* human parent, His mother; His Father being God. And the question as to the Person of Christ, which Christianity, in presence of modern scepticism in the garb of science, is necessitated to submit to Biology is this: Was it not possible for Him on the organic side of His being and life to owe His existence to no human parent unless His mother? That is to say, putting the question in its general form and in terms of Biology, Is it not possible for a human individual to begin his organic existence according to the Biological law of Agamogenesis instead of the law of Gamogenesis? There is only one answer that Biology can give to the question, and that is the reply: It was, or is possible. Thanks to Biology itself, Christianity is now in a position to be able to demand this reply from the Biologist as the only just one that can be given. Nor will any Biologist be so willing to concede

the reply as the one who most fully comprehends the meaning of certain orders of organic phenomena embraced by his science; and who is, consequently, deeply sensible of at least some of those mysteries of life which rest like a cloud of darkness on every organic being, from the moment when the first dawn of life appears till the moment when the last symptom of life dies away.

252. In order to prove its right to the reply just indicated, all that Christianity has to do is to appeal to Biology on the ground of certain organic phenomena as witnesses between them; witnesses supplied by Biology and worthy of its deference. The testimony of each of those witnesses in particular, and much more the combined testimony of all, is that the Biologist believes in the occurrence of events during the history of organic nature, each of which is Biologically more miraculous or marvellous than the organic occurrence that arose at the beginning of the Incarnation. We shall ask for the testimony of only a few of those witnesses; the testimony of any one of them by itself being quite sufficient to support the Biological possibility of the fundamental occurrence of Christianity. In this occurrence there is less to wonder at from the point of view of the Biologist than there is in any one of the following facts :—

First, There is the simple fact of the origination of life.

Second, There is the fact that all organic beings have a material basis worked into them from the inorganic world; and consisting of a few substances variously composed, of which carbon, oxygen, hydrogen, and nitrogen are among the most essential.

Third, There is the fact that one fundamental type of organic cells exists which develops into plants, and another fundamental type which develops into animals.

Fourth, There is the further fundamental fact that both in the sub-kingdom of plants and in the sub-kingdom of animals, there are special types of organic cells which develop respectively into special types of plants and animals.

Fifth, There is the fact that every perfect organism is a product of one of those Physiological units, and the fact that the course of organic development proceeds in different cases in *fundamentally different ways*.

Sixth, There is the fact that there are several *fundamentally unlike* ways according to which, in different cases, organic beings are reproduced in the course of nature.

253. What, then, is the significance of those facts with reference to our argument? Meanwhile it is only as facts that we have to consider them. They are all facts which have arisen during the history of organic nature. Every one of them as it came into existence was something original and new in the organic world. And there is not one of them, the coming into existence of which does not imply the existence of Biological possibilities in connection with its origin far greater and far more marvellous than those required to account for the entrance of the Son of God into His individual organic existence.

THE INCARNATION AND THE BIOLOGIST.

254. The Biologist has more to do with such organic phenomena, as those now specified, than simply to observe them. He has also to endeavour to account for them. He must ask, How did these marvellous facts come into existence? In attempting to answer this question, he must proceed on one or other of two principles—that of special acts of Creation, or that of Evolution. The Biologist, then, whichever of these two principles he adopts, whether he is a Creationist or an Evolutionist, must admit, in view of the facts which require to be explained, that the Incarnation was Biologically possible.

255. *First*, The Creationist. The Biologist who believes in the occurrence of special acts of creation during the history of organic phenomena, might object to the possibility of the Incarnation on other than Biological grounds. But in this case his words could not be regarded as possessing any scientific value, as they have such value only when he speaks in the name of his own special

science alone. It is only by what he says as a Biologist that the argument for the Biological possibility of the Incarnation can be affected. And as a Creationist he is, of course, bound to take up a position in favour of the argument. He admits that by special acts of creative power such organic facts as we have learnt from him, and have pointed out above, were brought into existence; and he knows that the Incarnation, viewed as resulting from a Biological act of Divine power, is less marvellous, or at least not more marvellous, than any one of those facts.

256. *Second*, The Evolutionist. So far as the *facts* are concerned, there is no difference between the Evolutionist and the Creationist. The former differs from the latter only in his way of explaining the facts. The Evolutionist believes that the facts exist, that they came into existence during the course of organic nature, and that they originated from adequate causes. He believes, that is to say, that causes existed as forms of efficiency in nature, capable of originating such organic phenomena as life and the fundamentally different types of Physiological cells, etc. And that implies belief in the occurrence of events by way of Evolution more astonishing by far than the one for which we are contending. Nor does it matter what view the Evolutionist takes of the nature of the causation from which new organic phenomena arise. He may believe in the existence of a personal God, and of His immanent and constant efficiency in nature. Or he may believe that there is no Divine personal cause at work in nature, and that, consequently, all new organic phenomena arise from the action of natural forces. Still he has such new Biological facts to account for as those which have been introduced into our argument. And if it is possible for him to account for any one of these facts by his principle, much more must the same principle permit him to believe in the possibility of an exceptional instance of Agamogenesis.

257. But the compatibility of the Incarnation with organic Evolution is seen also from other points of view. From the principle of Evolution and certain Biological phenomena, an

argument might be drawn even in favour of that event. If the theory of Evolution were proved to be more worthy of being accepted than that of special creations, it would not be very difficult to reconcile the Incarnation and the great subsequent facts and the future destiny of Christianity with it. This, of course, does not in the least prove the theory of Evolution to be true, and its rival theory false. It only proves, and it is well for this to be noted, that Christianity has nothing to fear from it. Let us examine this a little.

ORGANIC EVOLUTION FAVOURS THE INCARNATION.

258. The theory of Evolution, as applied to Biological phenomena, sets before us several groups of salient facts. (1) According to the theory, organic Evolution has proceeded gradually upwards from lower to higher forms of organic beings, the last species in the order of the series being man. (2) Viewed in another way, it is observed that Evolution has proceeded upwards from chemical substances to bioplasm, from bioplasm to cells, from cells to organisms, and from organs of a lower to organs of a higher type. (3) Again, from still another point of view, it is seen that Evolution has proceeded upwards from insensibility to sensation; from sensation to instinct; from instinct to self-consciousness, thought, self-determination, sentiments of right and wrong, and of obligation and responsibility.

259. The question is forced upon us, then, with these facts before us: Has the process of Evolution ceased in the organic world? Has it added the last link to its chain? Or is Evolution still in process in organic nature? And if it is impossible for the process to evolve a higher order of organic beings than man, are there not still in him personal and social spiritual possibilities, capable of being evolved into types of phenomena higher than any hitherto manifested *as fixed and general* in the human race? May it not be the case that the natural in humanity generally, if not universally, is undergoing a process of Evolution

into the spiritual? Is it not possible for man, in all the members of the race, and throughout the entire bounds of society, to be completely regenerated, and to be so elevated by spiritual attainments as to conform to the spiritual type of manhood presented in the earthly life of the Son of Man? The history of organic phenomena, as interpreted by the principle of Evolution, seems to suggest two conclusions: (1) That there is no ground whatsoever for assuming that the process of Evolution has completely exhausted itself and come to an end; (2) That if the process is to be continued, as we have reason to believe it will be, it will be continued in the higher region of man's *spiritual life*. We have no evidence from Biology that there is any upward tendency towards a higher plane of being and life, manifesting itself in any of the species or classes of animals below man. Moreover, no hint is forthcoming to lead us to expect upon the scene of the organic world any new species of beings higher than that of the human race. But, on the other hand, the entire course of human history, the gradual but certain upward tendency of civilisation from lower to higher levels, and the increasing acceleration of this tendency in the present century, is evidence sufficient that man is on his way towards a loftier spiritual destiny. He is being transformed from a lower into a higher type of being.

260. But, according to the principle of Evolution, every new type of being that arises and becomes general and fixed, must have an adequate cause to originate it and to control it during the process of its evolution. The Incarnation then fulfils this requirement of the principle. As the new and perfect type of the spiritual man, Christ appeared in history. He was the God-Man, the Son of Man, the second Adam. He became one with man to make man one with God. "The first Adam became a living soul. The last Adam became a life-giving spirit. Howbeit that is not first which is spiritual, but that which is natural, then that which is spiritual. The first man is of the earth, earthy: the second man is of heaven. As is the earthy, such are they

also that are earthy : and as is the heavenly, such are they also that are heavenly. And as we have borne the image of the earthy, we shall also bear the image of the heavenly" (1 Cor. xv. 45-49).

261. Finally, the possibility of the Incarnation and its actual occurrence are in perfect accordance with all the other conclusions at which we have already arrived ; conclusions as to God's relation to nature, as to natural law and natural laws, and as to natural force and its capabilities and incapabilities. And, therefore, we feel certain that the more science cares to consider the Biological import of the Incarnation, and the more it understands its own principles and its own conclusions regarding natural law and natural force, the more ready will it be to acknowledge that the Incarnation was an event which might happen. But there are other questions concerning this great event which we must now proceed to examine. Was the event necessary? And did it actually occur? The one question must be answered by religion, the other by religion and history. And if religion and history can furnish reasonable grounds on which the Incarnation may be regarded as a necessity and as a fact, then it devolves on men of science to regard faith in the Divinity of Christ as consistent with culture and worthy of honour.

CHAPTER XIV.

THE INCARNATION NECESSARY.—RELIGION.

Preliminary. The Incarnation and its Metaphysical Possibility. The Incarnation and its Ethical Possibility. Mode of Inquiry as to the Necessity for it. The Incarnation and Law. The Incarnation and *Final* Causation: (1) The Incarnation and Man's Spiritual Needs— (2) The Incarnation designed to meet those needs—What is Christianity and the true Evangelical?—(3) The Incarnation a way to meet those needs. The Incarnation and *Efficient* Causation: God's Love as Grace required the Incarnation to give it adequate Power—God's Love leads to the Incarnation—God's Grace and Christ's Person—God's Grace and Christ's Personal History—God's Grace and Christ's Self-sacrifice— God's Grace and Christ's Sufferings. Christ as the Power of God in Effect: Sin and Man's spiritual relations to God and to his brother— Christ's Power in its effect on God—Christ's Power in its effect on Man, in His Character as Revealer, Reconciler, Redeemer.

262. From the possibility of the Incarnation we now pass to consider the *necessity* for it. The question of possibility, as has been shown, is one which no science, unless that of Biology, is qualified to examine. And this science cannot escape from admitting that the Incarnation *may* be a fact, since it admits the existence of other facts still more difficult to account for when viewed in relation to the course of nature. Hence, if it can be shown on religious and moral grounds that the Incarnation was necessary, and still more if it can be shown that Christ, considered historically, meets all the religious and moral requirements of the person and life of one both Divine and human, then it follows that science is chargeable either with unreasonableness or presumption, in so far as it may deny or discredit the fact that the Man Christ Jesus was the eternal Son of God.

263. The Person of Christ involves Metaphysical as well as Biological questions as to possibility. But the possibility of the Incarnation on its Metaphysical side is assumed by the Christian Scriptures with unbroken silence. It has often been overlooked that the Bible, as containing a Divine revelation, was never intended to solve any question purely scientific. But it has perhaps been still oftener lost sight of that it was as little intended to solve any question purely Metaphysical.

264. This revelation was given solely for saving, religious, and moral purposes. And what the Christian Scriptures seek to show is that the Incarnation was necessary for these purposes, and that it became a fact.

265. The Ethical possibility of the Incarnation is quite apparent. In this respect it was possible on the human side, because man was made in the image of God. And on the Divine side it was possible, because the glory of God consists in His moral perfections, and especially in His holy love.

266. Let us then inquire into the necessity for the Incarnation, and as to method, or points of view from which to do so, let us accept suggestions from some words of Paul with reference to Christ. According to his teaching Christ was Divine, and Christ crucified is the power of God and the wisdom of God; and He is this because the grace of God abounds in Him towards men as sinners. Let us take these three ideas: Christ the *wisdom* of God; Christ the *power* of God; and the *grace* of God; and while making use of them we shall find our way to the cross of Christ, where they are all manifested to the utmost of their splendour and significance.

267. Some laws, we have seen, are common both to the natural world and to the spiritual world. And if our knowledge were free from all limitations, we should doubtless be able to frame special orders of spiritual laws to which all the different kinds of phenomena in the spiritual world could be referred. And we may assume that the Incarnation, which is one of the greatest facts in

the spiritual world, as it is one of the greatest facts in the natural world, happened in accordance with spiritual laws. Nay, rather we know that it did happen in accordance with such laws. And science should be all the more ready to support and honour belief in the fact of the Incarnation, because those laws are at the same time so universal in the natural world that no single exception to them is known to exist. What are those laws? They are two. Christ as the *wisdom* of God implies a classification of the fact of the Incarnation under the law of *Final Causation*; and Christ as the *power* of God implies a classification of the same fact under the law of *Efficient* Causation. And that which makes it possible for Christ as the God-Man to be classified under both of those laws is the circumstance that in Him, and especially in Him as crucified, the love of God as grace has appeared to men as sinners. Let us then try to see how the Incarnation happened in accordance (1) with the law of Final Causation, and (2) with the law of Efficient Causation.

THE INCARNATION AND FINAL CAUSATION.

268. In explaining the necessity for the Incarnation under the law of Final Causation, we must keep in mind that the Person of Christ is to be taken in its connection with His life, His death, and His entire work. In obedience to this law, then, God adopted the Incarnation as means towards certain ends.

269. *First*, It is to be noted that Christ is the wisdom of God with reference to man's *spiritual needs*. So far as known to us, man's spiritual needs are far higher in their importance than any other order of needs in him or in the creatures beneath him. Those needs include not only such as concern his own private interests, but also such as concern him in relation to other persons, to society, and to God. But what are man's spiritual needs? (1) As a sinner he is in need of salvation from sin. (2) As man he is in need of religion. (3) As man also he is in need of morality. And it is to be noted that a distinction is here drawn between

what man is in need of as a *sinner* and what he is in need of as *man*. For he would have had need of religion and morality although he had never become a sinner at all. Sin, and consequently deliverance from sin, are quite accidental to him. But as man he has been made, in the constitution of his spiritual nature, both for God and for his brother; for which reason, and apart altogether from sin, both religion and morality have a place among his essential and eternal needs. But inasmuch as he is a sinner, he is without both religion and morality in the spiritual and true sense of these terms; and continues without them until, through a new and absolutely necessary spiritual birth, he has begun to die unto sin and live unto righteousness.

270. The Incarnation, then, as coming under the law of Finality, had regard to all those needs. Its object was to meet them all, and to meet each of them completely. And if we would see Christ as the wisdom of God, we must not only take them into consideration, but also understand them. We cannot understand the wisdom represented by any fact or person as related to certain ends, until we understand at least the nature and the significance of those ends.

271. *Second*, But the Incarnation is also to be considered as representing a *design* to meet all those spiritual needs in man. And when considered in this aspect also it still further commends itself as Divine wisdom. The purpose of the Incarnation is the purpose of Christianity. But what is Christianity? what is it intended to be? Much more, let us gladly acknowledge, than it often gets credit for being from some of those who put themselves forward as its zealous advocates. Christianity is intended to meet *all* man's spiritual needs, and not one of them only; and to meet each of them to the utmost. It was never designed by Divine wisdom that it should be one thing only, say, a mode of deliverance from human guilt and Divine wrath; or, say, a form of religion; or, say, a system of moral maxims and precepts. Man would have needed Christianity as eternal life, as perfect spiritual life towards God and towards his brother, he would, in other

words, have needed two-thirds of Christianity, although deliverance from sin had never been required by him. And, on the other hand, since he has become a sinner, he not only needs deliverance from sin, but until this has been obtained and he has personally entered into the state of deliverance, he cannot have that eternal life, that perfect spiritual life towards God and his brother, that Christianity has provided for him.

272. And thus it will appear what Christianity is and was intended to be. In point both of purpose and of fitness, it is at once an all-sufficient mode of deliverance from sin for man as a sinner; and the absolute, universal, eternal religion for man as man; and the absolute, universal, eternal morality for man as man. It is all these three in one. And it is the last two because it is the first. The deliverance from sin is the means, and the religion and the morality are the end. Christianity seeks to save man from sin, and that even now as far as possible. It seeks by means of his deliverance from sin to bring him as far as possible even now into a life of true spiritual religion towards God; and it seeks this as a present consequence from his deliverance from the guilt and power of moral evil. And, lastly, it seeks to bring man, in consequence of this new spiritual relation to God, into a life of true spiritual morality towards his brother. And as Christianity sets before it this threefold aim; and as the three particular objects, salvation, religion, morality, are all essential and necessary elements of the one great purpose of the wisdom of God in Christ, which has respect to all man's spiritual needs, that teaching alone deserves the name of *Evangelical*, in the true and complete sense of the term, which pays explicit and full respect to all the elements of this manifold wisdom of God. This threefold purpose of Christianity, then, is one of its most distinctive features and one of its special glories, and the more this purpose in its various aspects and bearings on man's spiritual needs becomes comprehended, the more will it appear that it is not without most profound reasons that the Incarnation is ranked under the Law of Finality.

K

273. *Third*, There is, however, another way in which the Incarnation fulfils the Law of Finality. The Divine wisdom represented by the Incarnation has regard to all man's spiritual needs, and it seeks to meet them. But how does it propose to meet them? It proposes to meet one and all of them by means of the *grace* of God in Christ: not the love of God simply; but the love of God as grace; the love of God, that is, to the ill-deserving. The Incarnation is a plan adopted by God in His wisdom, by means of which He has sought to manifest His gracious saving love to men as sinners; and to bring this love into complete and eternal effect in meeting all their spiritual needs as sinners and as men. And from this point of view we are specially enabled to comprehend why Christ should have been designated the wisdom of God.

274. The entire problem of man's spiritual needs—his need of salvation from sin, his need of religion, and his need of morality—is solved, and completely solved, in Christ. And the entire solution lies in the holy and gracious love of God which has appeared in the Person of Christ as the God-Man, and which has been manifested in His life and in His cross, but especially in His cross. Man as a sinner needs the gracious love of God brought to him in personal salvation. As man he needs to love God. And as man he needs to love his brother. And the perfect wisdom of God in Christ appears in this, that Christ saves the believing sinner by means of the grace of God; and thereby constrains him to love God with holy love; and thereby, again, constrains him to love his brother with holy love. In other words, the wisdom of God has purposed, by means of His gracious love revealed in Christ, to save men from their sin, and to bring them, through this saving love to them, into the fellowship of a life of perfect love to God and to one another in Christ, " That they may all be one; even as Thou, Father, art in me, and I in Thee; that they also may be one in us."

275. In all these respects, then, the necessity for the Incarnation appears under the form of Divine wisdom, and as a marvellous

instance of obedience to the Law of Final Causation. But the necessity for it will appear still more impressively when we have considered it with reference to the Law of Efficient Causation.

THE INCARNATION AND EFFICIENT CAUSATION.

276. The Incarnation was necessary to give efficiency to the gracious love of God in its threefold purpose to meet man's spiritual needs. The gracious love of God could not have acted as an adequate efficient cause in meeting those needs apart from the Incarnation. Science has given us the law of the Transformation of natural energy. And there is such a thing as the transformation of spiritual energy. The love of God is spiritual energy; and His love is capable of being transformed as to its mode of self-manifestation. The love of God as love simple, is not absolutely the same as His love when manifested in the form of grace. The idea of Divine grace, according to Christianity, presupposes the existence of sin. Divine love cannot manifest itself as grace, unless with reference to sin, and the ill-desert which it implies. Had sin never existed, God would have been perfect love. But His love could never have been known in the form of grace; since all the personal beings loved by Him would have been worthy to receive His love. The existence of sin in man has, however, so far as he is concerned, created new conditions for the love of God to deal with. And all God's love to man as a sinner is transformed Divine love; it is Divine love with the new character of grace. And if man is to be saved from sin, and have all his other spiritual needs met by the love of God, this Divine love must transform itself into the form of grace, and it must manifest itself as acting in the form of grace. And what we have now to show is that the Incarnation was necessary as a way whereby the love of God might be sufficiently changed into the form of grace, and invested with adequate power to effect all its designs with reference to man's spiritual needs.

277. *First*, Let us begin with the observation that the Incarna-

tion as a fact came into existence from the action of God's *love* seeking to carry out its designs. The ultimate necessity for the Incarnation lay in His love. Whether His love would have necessitated the Incarnation, supposing sin never to have existed, is a question which need not be examined. In the Christian Scriptures the Incarnation is connected with the love of God on the one hand, and with the condition of man as a sinner and his spiritual needs on the other. And we are on sure ground only when we consider the necessity for the Incarnation from this point of view. The gracious love of God, then, necessitated the Incarnation in view of man's spiritual needs. "The Word became flesh and dwelt among us; and we beheld His glory, the glory as of the Only-begotten of the Father, full of grace and truth. . . . God so loved the world that He gave His only-begotten Son. . . . Herein is love, not that we loved God, but that He loved us, and sent His Son." That which necessitated the love of God to send His Son in the nature of man was His gracious purpose and the spiritual conditions required to effect it. Before His love could meet man's spiritual needs it required to be manifested as grace and clothed with gracious saving power; it required to be revealed in action as a gracious and adequate redeeming efficiency.

278. *Second*, But we must now go on to see why the love of God as grace required the Incarnation; and it is to be noted, in the first place, that it required the *Person* of Christ as the God-Man to enable it to meet man's spiritual needs. Before it could act to the utmost of its power in meeting those needs, it was under the necessity of appearing in a person, and as acting through his personality. The love of God as grace never could have invested itself with all the power possible to it by expressing itself in mere words; even although words spoken by a prophet, or by Christ Himself. The proper medium for the manifestation of love is personality and individual life; and the love manifested must appear not as speaking only, but as acting. Obviously, then, the grace of God required the Person of Christ as the God-Man as a fit medium through which to reveal itself in action. He

alone as Divine could reveal it in all its trueness and fulness. And yet, at the same time, as human, He could reveal it acting in all its intensity and plenitude within the limits of an individual life in the world.

279. *Third*, The love of God as grace, moreover, required the Incarnation because it was under the necessity of acting, and of manifesting itself in *History*. The life of Christ in its historical meaning and power was as necessary as His Person, if man's spiritual needs were to be met. If those needs were to be met, God's gracious love could no more do without a historical medium than it could without a personal medium. Even Christ could not have met them without taking a place in history as the God-Man, and living an individual life such as history could claim as its own, and in as true a sense as it can claim that of any mere man whose name is written on its pages, and whose individual influence has left a mark on its character. A God-Man, living and dying alone, out of all social and public relations with men, quite unknown, and therefore, in effect, entirely unhistorical, never could have possessed the qualifications requisite to make Him the Light of the world, and the Saviour of the lost. The gracious love of God, consequently, embodied itself, acted, and manifested itself in the history as well as in the Person of Christ. And it did this because otherwise it could not have provided itself with such conditions as are required to transform it into the plenitude of its redeeming power.

280. *Fourth*, God's gracious love required the Incarnation also because it could not have met all man's spiritual needs without appearing and acting in history by means of a life of perfect *self-sacrifice*. It could no more have met man's spiritual needs without a life of perfect self-sacrifice, than it could have met them without appearing in personal and historical action. It therefore provided the life of perfect self-sacrifice that was lived by Christ, the God-Man. He had the gracious love of God embodied in His personality. He transformed this Divine love into His life; and, in particular, He revealed it in the form of complete self-surrender

and self-devotion to those whose spiritual needs He had come to meet. Nor is it possible, may it not be asserted? for any one to conceive of God's love as grace, taking upon itself any form of self-sacrifice for its objects more complete and more impressive than that which from first to last, and on all occasions, was acted out and displayed by Christ. He lived and died on the principle that He had not come to be ministered unto, but to minister and to give His life a ransom for many. When He said, "I am the Good Shepherd, the Good Shepherd giveth His life for the sheep," He spoke in the name of Divine grace in its perfect self-sacrifice as the ruling power in His life. Nor did He mean only that He was soon to lay down His life in death for the objects of Divine grace; for laying down His life for them was the principle of His living as well as of His dying. Laying down His life was with Him to take His life, His life from His earliest years to His last moments, His life with all its incarnate capabilities, and to consecrate it entirely to the purposes of Divine grace; that is, to meet the spiritual needs of men.

281. *Fifth*, God's love as grace also required the Incarnation in order that it might act and manifest itself as acting under *conditions of suffering*. It never could have been revealed in all its capabilities as grace, if it had not appeared acting for men as sinners under conditions of suffering, and conditions of the most trying nature. Self-sacrifice is a poor word to employ if it is meant thereby to express all that the gracious love of God did as it appeared in Christ. Love presented in the form of mere self-sacrifice is not love in its highest state of action and manifestation. To true moral love, self-sacrifice is not in itself a trial, but rather a condition of self-gratification and joy. Nor is moral love subjected to the highest possible test when it has simply to suffer for the sake of its objects. That which puts the mightiest strain upon such love is when its very self-sacrifice brings its suffering upon it; and when the suffering is inflicted by those very persons who are the objects of its devotion, and inflicted by them with ingratitude and malignity.

282. The gracious love of God in Christ, then, was tried in this manner, and tried to the utmost. He laid down His life in living, and He laid it down in dying. He drank the cup which His Father put into His hand, although His last struggle to accept it cost Him the bloody sweat of Gethsemane. He became obedient unto death, even the death of the cross. And by His perfect self-sacrifice, by His complete and free submission to His Father's will, and by His gracious patience during His Passion, He transformed His cross, as the consummation of His life, into the *power of God*.

283. But the question here arises, To what *effect* is Christ the power of God—Christ in His personality, in His life, in His teaching, in His death, and in His entire work as the Incarnate One?

CHRIST AS THE POWER OF GOD IN EFFECT.

284. Christ's power has reference to existing relations between God and man, and between man and man. Those relations are all spiritual in their nature; and the object of Christ's power is to rectify them. They stand in need of rectification, because sin as a disturbing element has come between man and God, and between man and man. Sin has spiritually separated man from God, and it has caused a spiritual separation of one man from another. And as spiritual disability is one of the characteristics of the state of those under the power of sin, some spiritual power superior to any possessed by man himself as a sinner is required to act as an adequate cause to remove sin from between him and God, and from between him and his brother. Christ, then, is the spiritual power required. And He alone is able to save man from sin, and to rectify all the spiritual relations just indicated.

285. The power of God in Christ is Divine power working *outwards* in relation to man, and seeking to introduce into his nature and life a spiritual force sufficient to secure his personal deliverance from sin, and his personal attainment of his spiritual

destiny. But this does not imply that the power of God in Christ did not or does not in some respects act, so to speak, *backwards* upon God Himself, producing some effect upon Him in His relation to men as sinners. All God's spiritual perfections exist in Him as *one* character, and essentially as a spirit He is Holy Love. But while the Divine love is capable of being transformed into grace towards the sinner, it is and must be transformed into anger against sin. Hence in its relation to men as sinners, the holy love of God is necessarily self-determined into the conflicting aspects of grace and anger, and hence the holy love of God in its relation to men as sinners demands an internal self-reconciliation. This reconciliation, then, Christ as the Incarnate One has effected. Through His Person as the God-man, and through His life and death as an atoning sacrifice for sin, He has reconciled the anger with the grace of God as a God of holy love, and as related to men as sinners. And now, with all the demands of His holy love as wrath against sin met, God is in Christ reconciling the world unto Himself, not reckoning unto them their trespasses. Nor is it possible to conceive how such a reconciliation of the conflicting aspects of God's holy love as both grace and anger at the same time, and, consequently, the reconciliation of God to sinners, ever could have been effected by any person save Christ, the God-Man ; One who not in His death only, but also in His person and in His life, in His entire self-manifestation and work, could occupy the place of a perfect substitute ; a substitute in God's place in relation to man, and in man's place in relation to God.

286. But Christ is also the power of God, as a God of holy love acting *outwards* in relation to man. And in effect Christ is the power of a perfect revelation of God's holy and gracious love ; and He is at the same time the power of a perfect reconciliation on the part of the sinner to God ; and withal He is the power of perfect personal redemption from sin, in consequence of which also He is the power of eternal life.

287. *First*, Christ is the power of God in His character as the *Revealer* of God's love. Two aspects of the revelation of God's love in Christ seem to be indisputable,—one is that no higher revelation of it can be imagined; and the other is that man even as a sinner can never require any higher revelation of it to meet the necessities of his condition. In Christ the love of God is revealed in all the perfection of its holy anger against sin, and at the same time it is revealed in all its perfection as grace towards sinners. In His own personality, in His life, in His words and works, in His death, by means of His complete self-sacrifice, and by means of the infinite patience of His obedience under suffering, He has so revealed God's love as grace to sinners, and as wrath against sin, that no further revelation of either the one or the other aspect of God's holy love seems to be possible. This revelation, then, is Divine power. And must not He who is this power be Divine — the God-Man?

288. *Second*, Christ is the power of God in His character as the *Reconciler* of sinners to God. In this respect Christ as power awakens sinners to feel their need of reconciliation to Him. Nor is there any power to be compared with His in its might to effect this result. As revealing the grace and the wrath of the love of God, and especially as revealing them in His cross, He stands alone as a spiritual power, and infinitely above every mere man known to have existed; convincing sinners of sin and guilt, and of their need of reconciliation to God; and doing this not only by means of the Divine anger revealed in Him against sin, but also, and perhaps still more, by means of the Divine grace manifested in Him to the chief of sinners. Besides, as a reconciling power, He brings the sinner into the presence of a God whose holy love has been harmonized in its conflicting requirements, and perfectly satisfied; the anger of whose love has been turned away, and the grace of whose love is free to bestow the blessing of absolute forgiveness and peace. Thus in Christ

are provided all the spiritual conditions and all the spiritual force necessary both to cause the sinner to realize his need of being reconciled to God, and to effect his reconciliation. And that it is so has been found by every sinner who has come spiritually under the power of Christ, and who in the spirit of repentance and faith has met God in Him. And such is the nature of the reconciliation thus effected, that it implies a grateful and loving appropriation of the free and forgiving grace of God in Christ; and this implies, again, or is concurrent with, a new and strong personal reaction against sin, which means hatred of it, and in a sense death to it. Such a reconciliation to God, men as sinners need. No one would even allow himself to believe for a moment that such a reconciliation could be effected in him by the spiritual power of any mere man. Paul, and all who have entered into his Christian ideas of faith and experience, have known that the power required to reconcile sinners to God must have in it Divine personality and worth. And so they have felt persuaded that Christ the Reconciler is the God-Man.

289. *Third*, Christ is the power of God in His character as the *Redeemer*. Man's spiritual needs have not all been completely met in Him personally, and in connection with his personal return to God and to his brother, until the element of sin has been entirely separated from him and he has entered upon a life of fellowship with God in Christ. This, then, is one of the ways in which the redeeming power of Christ takes effect. It not only causes the sinner to die unto sin, but in doing this it causes him to begin living unto God. And it does this all the more effectually because the redeeming power of Christ is essentially the power of redeeming *grace*. The idea of redeeming grace in Christ is the fundamental idea of Pauline Christianity. And it is this power of redeeming grace which, through the work of the Spirit on the heart, becomes a new inward spiritual force in the sinner reconciled to God, constraining him to love God in Christ, and thereby constraining him to love his brother also. The power

of Divine redeeming grace is the power of eternal life. No other power than this is competent to bring force enough to bear upon men to lead them into their true life towards God and towards one another. No other power equals this when it gets hold of men to lift them up out of a life of passion and impulse into a life of reason and faith. No other power save this is mighty enough to make moral love to God and to man universal among men; to reconcile every human will to the will of God; to unite heart to heart all over the world, and life to life, by the principle of self-renunciation and self-devotion, each man in this way spending his life for others, and in this way winning it back again as an eternal blessing.

290. In other words, no other power but the power of the redeeming grace of God in Christ is competent to bring on an answer to the prayer, "Our Father, which art in heaven. Hallowed be Thy name. Thy kingdom come. Thy will be done, as in heaven, so on earth." One thing certain is that a full and lasting answer to that prayer is what man's life, above all things, needs. And another thing certain is that the answer will never come, can never come, unless by way of the increasing entrance of the power of Divine redeeming grace into man's life, and the entrance of it in such a manner as to become a new regenerating spiritual force, constraining men gladly to imitate the grace of the Lord Jesus Christ. This being so, then, the Incarnation was required in the interests of sinful men and for the purposes of the redeeming grace of God.

CHAPTER XV.

THE INCARNATION VERIFIED.—RELIGION AND HISTORY.

> The Nature of the Inquiry. Christ's Life as Human was spiritually Perfect: The Records of His Life—General Statements as to His spiritual Perfection—His Life as Human in its spiritual Relation to God—His Life as Human in its spiritual Relation to Men—Christ as related to Himself through His Conduct—A Qualification. Christ was the eternal Son of God: (1) His spiritual Perfection as Man proves Him to be Divine—(2) His Claim to be the Son of God, taken with His spiritual Perfection, proves His Divinity—(3) His Divinity proved by the effect of His Personality on the Mind—(4) God's Love as revealed in Him proves Him to be Divine—(5) The effect of Christ's Love in men proves Him to be Divine.

291. We have learnt from Biology that there was a natural possibility for the Incarnation, and we have learnt from religion that it was necessary. Now, with the help of religion and history, we have to consider whether it is a fact? Was the Son of Man also the eternal Son of God? If Christ's Person had the originality claimed for Him by the doctrine of the Incarnation, there must have been a corresponding originality in His life. If He was both Divine and human, His life must have presented a revelation of His Divinity; and it must have been a life of human *spiritual* perfection. We have consequently two questions to answer, and it is well to keep them apart. (1) Was Christ's life on earth perfect in all its spiritual aspects and attainments as a human life? and (2) Was there in His life an appropriate and adequate revelation of His Divinity? If these two questions can

be answered in the affirmative and beyond all reasonable dispute, then it will be evident that the Incarnation which we have seen to be necessary must have become a fact.

CHRIST'S LIFE AS HUMAN SPIRITUALLY PERFECT.

292. If Christ was the Son of God Incarnate, He must have lived a life *spiritually perfect in all its human features and relations*. The discovery of one spiritual imperfection in Him, if sufficiently verified, would overthrow faith in His Divine claims. Whether or not the life which He did live as man was one of spiritual perfection, is a question which can be answered only from the records of His life contained in the four Gospel-narratives. It is to these records that we must appeal, and we may appeal to them assured that they are sufficient for our purpose, and that they are absolutely trustworthy. They deserve our confidence, because they force upon us the conviction that the life of Christ must have been lived as they sketch it for us. For if the life sketched had never been so lived as a fact, it never could have been so sketched as a fiction.

293. In seeking to show that Christ *as man* lived a life of spiritual perfection, it is, of course, on the spiritual side of His inner life and of His conduct that we must fix our attention. God sent forth His Son, born of a woman, under the law. Though the Son of God, Christ was bone of our bone, and flesh of our flesh. He lived and grew up and fulfilled the objects of His mission under the ordinary conditions and limitations of human life. He gained personal experience of toil, of weariness, of intercourse with friends, of dealings with enemies, of joys and sorrows, of encouragements and disappointments. He can be touched with a feeling of our infirmities ; for he was in all points tempted like as we are. And yet He was without sin. Nor was He innocent simply. He was positively holy ; completely perfect in His inward attitude, and in His endeavours with respect to all the spiritual prohibitions and requirements that rested upon His

life. When He called Himself the Son of Man, as He generally did, one of His reasons must have been the fact, of which He was conscious, that the life He lived was spiritually the ideal—the true, the absolute, the eternal—life proper to man as a spiritual being; proper to every member of the human race. Our question then is: Did He, indeed, during His life on earth fulfil all those spiritual requirements, entire conformity to which would constitute human perfection? We shall see that He did. There was not one of them which He did not fulfil; and every one of them He fulfilled to the highest possible degree of perfection. In order to see this, we have but to study and to understand Him as acting in all the spiritual relations of His life as the Son of Man; in His spiritual relation to God, in His spiritual relation to man, and in His spiritual relation to Himself.

294. *First*, Let us begin with His life as human in its *spiritual relation to God*. Man's spiritual relation to God is the highest of all the relations in his life. He has been made for God, and in His image; and his proper destiny is to possess and enjoy Him in a life of fellowship, and to live for Him a life of free and complete self-surrender and service. It is, then, one of the marvellous forms of spiritual perfection in Christ's life as man that, from first to last, He not only recognised this to be the supreme spiritual relation in His life, but lived in absolute conformity to all its requirements. His spiritual relation to God was always present to His mind, and uppermost in His thoughts, and all-determining as to His conduct. To study the records of His life, and not to discern that it was so, would be totally to misunderstand their spiritual significance. And it does not require to be affirmed that if His life within the sphere of its spiritual relation to God was a perfect life, His is the only human life regarding which any one would seriously predicate such perfection. But instead of dwelling on this form of His spiritual perfection in its general aspect only, let us resolve it into its minor features. What does man's spiritual relation to God involve?

295. (1.) Man's spiritual relation to God implies that he ought

to look to God alone as having absolute right to determine for him the purpose of his being and life.

(2.) Again, this relation implies that he ought to yield absolute submission to God's will in all its directions and requirements as to the way in which the life-purpose assigned should be realized.

(3.) Further, the relation implies that man requires and ought to live by complete and constant dependence on God for help to do His will, and to finish His work.

(4.) The relation, lastly, implies that he ought to make it his "meat," to reckon it his blessedness, to be entirely faithful to God's will and purpose for his life in all their requirements.

296. Christ, then, was human; and He proved Himself to be spiritually perfect in all these various aspects of the human relation to God. Not in one way only, but in every way, His life within this sphere was without sin. No sin can with truth and justice be imputed to Him here. The closer that truth and justice come to Him, and the more inwardly they inspect Him in His bearing towards God on all occasions, the more does the perfection of His holiness appear. Take Him in relation to God's purpose for His life, and you will find on examination how impossible it is ever to detect Him coming short of entire personal consecration. Again, take Him in relation to God's will for His life, and you will see on examination that He never once makes the slightest deviation from the path of perfect obedience. Then, take Him in relation to God's help for His life, and you will discover on examination how impossible it would be for any human being ever to trust in God with a more absolute confidence. Lastly, take Him in relation to His own joy, and the more He becomes understood by you, the more it will become apparent that His joy was perfect in its spirituality and strength. On no occasion did it ever arise from any worldly, from any unspiritual, consideration or impulse. On every occasion it was the pure and perfect joy of God; it was the joy He found in accomplishing God's work, in doing God's will, in fulfilling all righteousness.

297. Thus the Son of Man lived. Within this region of His

life the Prince of this world had nothing in Him. No one can approach Him here and convince Him of sin. He stands alone in the peerlessness of His spiritual perfection, separate from sinners. In this respect He is a spiritual miracle. No mere man has a right to claim classification with him in respect of this attainment. No mere man has ever proved himself to be worthy of such a classification. And personal unworthiness to be so classified, has never been so deeply felt and acknowledged as by those men who have been most successful in earnest and persistent endeavours and struggles to follow the Son of Man.

298. *Second,* We next come to Christ's life as human, in its *spiritual relation to men.* As the Son of Man, He completely identified Himself with human well-being. If ever there was a genuine and perfect interest taken in humanity, it was by Him. No one of sane mind, and free from prejudice, would ever for a moment doubt the reality of His love for men. It is manifest, too, that His love for men was spiritual in its nature and spiritual in all its modes of self-manifestation and action. And to see the reality of His love for men and to understand its spirituality, is, at the same time, to be convinced of its perfection. His constant and entire self-renunciation for the sake of men, and His constant and entire self-devotion to them and their spiritual and other human needs, met in the highest possible degree all the requirements of true and enlightened self-consecration to humanity. He went about doing good. He pleased not Himself. As the Son of Man He came, as He Himself testified, not to be ministered unto, but to minister, and to give His life a ransom for many. And as He testified, so He lived, and so He died. His enthusiasm for humanity was as constant and complete as His devotion to God; and in the one He proved Himself to be as perfectly holy as in the other. But here also let us enter into some particulars.

299. (1.) One evidence of Christ's spiritual perfection as man, in His relation to men, *is the unparalleled value that He attached to humanity, and the respect that He paid to it.* He spoke of one soul, one human life, as worth more than all the world. He

claimed to be the Son of God, and He proved the value that He set upon humanity and upon human life, by uniting man's nature with His Godhead and by living man's life as the Son of God. Besides, that He held human lives to be so precious, even although sinful and persisting in sin, was proved by the life that He lived and the death that He died for their salvation. And in His estimation every human life had the same value. He paid no respect to persons. He looked upon men with eyes of absolute impartiality. In His regard to men and in His judgment of them, all prejudice and bias were transcended. No accidental circumstance of social rank, or of wealth, or of official position and power, or even of blood-relationship, ever in the slightest degree affected His estimation of any human being.

300. One of the few occasions on which He has been supposed by some to have sinned, was when He seemed to despise the value of blood-relationship altogether. This was when He used words in which He seemed to renounce all the members of His family. He was told that His mother and His brethren sought to speak to Him. But, stretching out His hand towards the multitude, He replied, "Who is my mother, and who are my brethren? Behold my mother and my brethren! For whosoever shall do the will of my Father which is in heaven, he is my brother, and sister, and mother." But, in reality, what the Son of Man said on this occasion was not a proof of sin, but a proof rather of the entire impartiality and the perfect holiness of His enthusiasm for men, and a proof of the inestimable value that every man's soul had in His sight. We hold, then, that Christ as man was perfectly holy in His love for the souls, for the lives, of perishing men, and in His estimation of their worth.

301. (2.) Another aspect of His spiritual perfection as man appears in His *compassion for men*. Why was He a man of sorrows? There is only one answer possible to this question, the answer, viz., that as the Son of Man He was man's brother and friend, and that He had the feeling of perfect spiritual brotherhood towards him. All the woes and miseries of

humanity were His woes and miseries. "Himself took our infirmities and bare our diseases." He possessed and manifested in all its perfection the power of sympathy with the needs and the physical and moral sufferings of man. Hence we are so often told that He was "moved with compassion." And hence, too, it was that He performed so many deeds of mercy. This compassion of His, then, was one of the elements of His spiritual perfection. His compassion for men was as perfect in holiness as His love to God.

302. (3.) But in His spiritual relation to men, Christ as man had to take up an attitude towards their *sin* as well as towards their misery. What attitude, then, did He take up? Did He prove Himself to be spiritually perfect here also? Most manifestly He did. He made a distinction in His treatment of sin between the sin and the sinner. He loved sinners not as sinners, but in spite of their being sinners. He had to bear the reproach of being their friend. They were drawn to Him in many instances by the very perfection of His holiness. And He never failed to show them mercy, and to forgive them, and send them away in peace, if they approached Him in penitence and faith. And yet, on the other hand, He was hostile to every form of sin. He had perfect insight into the nature of sin, into its meaning as rebellion against God, and into its meaning as a curse in the sinner's own life. By His teaching and by His own life, sin was absolutely condemned. He brought Himself to His cross by His exposure of sin, and by the bold and faithful reaction of His holiness against it. Let His attitude towards sin be studied in all its aspects, and it will be seen how perfect it was as a spiritual element in His life.

303. -(4.) But once more, Christ as man was spiritually perfect in His attitude towards *the true life that all men need*. He saw their need of eternal life as a present, and not only as a future blessing. It was His constant desire that men might have this life, and that they might have it abundantly. His whole life, His deeds, His discourses in public, His conversations in private,

all show how completely His mind was filled with pure, glowing, unwearied enthusiasm to get men to share with Him in that eternal and blessed life which so entirely satisfied His own being. His tears and lamentation over Jerusalem in its impenitence are an impressive testimony to this form of His spiritual perfection.

304. *Third*, Christ as man, while spiritually related to God and to man, was also *spiritually related to Himself through His conduct*. And in this respect also His life was one of spiritual perfection. His life was a life of perfect moral self-respect. No stain of sin or of moral dishonour was ever allowed to touch His humanity. He exalted His human nature and life to the highest possible honour by His perfect consecration of them to the purpose and will of God, and to the service of men. In Him the lower impulses of life were completely under the command of reason and conscience. His power to turn stones into bread was not entrusted to Him to meet His own hunger, and so He refused to employ it for this private end. Though He was so perfectly wise and humble, He never knew what it was to learn to be wise or humble through experience of yielding to temptation. Though He was so gracious and gentle to repenting sinners, He never Himself had occasion to repent. No occasion is ever presented in His life on which He had reason to feel regret or remorse for His words or actions. His life was one of inward, perfect peace. There was perfect and constant harmony among all the elements of His life within; and there was constant and perfect correspondence on His part with all the objects that determined Him in His life from without. He never showed, and never had cause to show, any sense of shortcoming in His life. His standard of spiritual perfection for man was the highest possible; and this standard was never above His own actual attainments at any moment or in any direction.

305. Thus as man Christ lived a spiritually perfect life. If we look at His life from the side of God, or from the

side of man, or from the side of Himself, and judge of it in the light of all that spiritual perfection demands, we see nothing anywhere but evidence of the perfection of His human holiness. But all the evidence which has been thus noticed requires some qualification to give it full significance.

A QUALIFICATION.

306. If Christ's spiritual perfection as man was never subjected to trial, it has one value; if it was reached or maintained under circumstances of temptation, it has another, and one higher beyond all computation. We must remember, consequently, that He was in all points tempted like as we are, and that He was made perfect through suffering. This fact adds immensely to the miraculous character of His spiritual perfection. The perfection of His holiness on its human side was glorified by temptations met and successfully overcome. It was the temptations He had to encounter, and the manner in which He triumphed over them, that brought His sinlessness into full manifestation before the eyes of men, and proved how strong in holiness He was. He was tempted and tried up to the highest conceivable measure in connection with His spiritual relation to God. It was by His constant and entire devotion to God's purpose and will that He was brought to His cross, with all its physical torture and its moral agony. Up to the highest possible point also He was tempted and tried in connection with His spiritual relation to men. From them He had to endure falsehood, hatred, malignity, treachery, disloyalty. And they brought upon themselves even the guilt of His blood. And yet He was without sin. The fires of His temptations had no other effect upon Him than to make all the various forms of His spiritual perfections shine forth in their full splendour and glory. It looks as if all that He required and had waited for were the final temptations and trials of His life,

as conditions under which to display how absolutely perfect His holiness was in His relation to God, to men, and to Himself.

CHRIST WAS THE ETERNAL SON OF GOD.

307. We now come to consider the question whether Christ was Divine. He was the Son of God as well as the Son of Man, according to the doctrine of the Incarnation.

308. *First,* What has already been proved and explained as to *the spiritual perfection of Christ's life as human, is itself, when rightly regarded, an indisputable testimony to His Divinity.* It is to be noticed again that the life of Christ, when considered as human, is a spiritual miracle. It stands alone in the history of spiritual attainment in human life. And it seems to be impossible to account for it, unless on the supposition that He had a Divine element in His personality. Anything original in a phenomenon implies something original in the cause by which it comes into existence. This holds good in the spiritual as well as in the natural world. And since the life of Christ in its spiritual attainments is an absolutely singular phenomenon in the spiritual world, and since His life arose as a fact from His personality, there must have been present in His personality some extraordinary cause, to which His extraordinary life must be referred. Noting this, then, and connecting it with other facts yet to be mentioned, we conclude that Christ must have been the Son of God. His Divinity is revealed to us in and through His humanity. His spiritual perfection as man is a reflection of His Divine glory. And this is why we have examined the human aspects of His life before considering the proofs of His Divinity. With His spiritual perfection as the Son of Man shining before our eyes, we have no alternative left but to acknowledge His claims to be the Son of God.

309. *Second.* The Divinity of Christ is proved by *His claim to*

be the Son of God. He did regard Himself as the Son of God, and required others to accept Him, to trust in Him, to obey Him, and to honour Him as such. The Father was in Him, and He was in the Father. He and the Father were one, and His claim to be Divine was so strong, that He said, "He that hath seen me hath seen the Father." But, then, the question arises, Might His claim not have been fanatical or false? Was He not carried away by a mistaken belief regarding Himself? Or, if not, did He not try to deceive the people? It is impossible to explain His claim either the one way or the other. Either alternative, owing to His spiritual perfection as human, implies an absolute moral contradiction. One of such spiritual attainments as His could never be self-deceived, nor could such an one ever attempt to deceive others. We have seen His absolute spiritual perfection as man on the one hand, and on the other, He meets us with the claim that He is the eternal Son of God; and we find it impossible not to admit that His claim must be true.

310. *Third,* Christ's Divinity receives further verification *from the effect of His personality and life on the heart.* It is to Christ that we have to turn when we desire to learn most truly what God is as a spiritual Being. Nor is it Christ's words only that reveal to us the Father; it is also and chiefly Christ Himself. We gain our highest conceptions of the glory of God from the face of Jesus Christ. How many men have been satisfied with Christ as God! They never knew God until they knew Him. After they knew Him it became impossible for them to think of God as greater or better than He. And so they have been persuaded that Christ must be Divine. And their persuasion has been strengthened in proportion as they have grown in acquaintance with Christ as known to them through the facts of His life and of His death; in proportion as they have entered into His Spirit; and in proportion as they have learnt how completely He could meet their spiritual needs in all possible circumstances.

311. *Fourth,* God is love, and it is in itself a conclusive proof of Christ's Divinity that *the love of God in all its fulness and per-*

fection has been revealed through His life and death to the world. Through Christ God has revealed His love to the world in two ways. (1) He has revealed it through Him inasmuch as He is the unspeakable gift of His love bestowed on men. But (2) He has also revealed it in Christ's own love to men. The love of Christ is the equivalent of the love of God. If Christ was not Divine, the love of God has not yet been adequately revealed to men. The world has never yet seen how much Divine love can surrender, and do, and suffer for men. Is it so? Christ is the answer. He has shown the world that God is love. Men have learnt, and they will never unlearn, to measure the greatness of Divine love by the spiritual greatness of Christ, and by the character and greatness of His love to the world.

312. The idea of God as love was unknown in the heathen world until Christ appeared. It is to Him that the Gentile nations are indebted for the knowledge of it. The gracious character of God, however, was known among the Jews. God, as revealed in the history of the Patriarchs and of the Jewish nation, the God of the Law and of the Prophets, was merciful and gracious, long-suffering, and slow to anger; while He was also a God of wrath. His holy love reacted in the form of wrath against sin in His people; and yet it pitied them when they sinned, and pleaded with them to repent, and was ready to forgive. But who has revealed to the world the God of the Old Testament in all the plenitude and glory of His holy love to men; and to men not as constituted into a people only, but to men as individuals? Christ has done it, and He alone. He has done it partly by means of His teaching. He has done it mostly by means of His personality; by means of Himself as the Truth, the Light of the world; Himself as revealed through all the circumstances of His life, and especially through all the circumstances of His death. Christ, and especially Christ crucified, is the supreme and all-sufficient revelation to men of God's holy love in its reaction under the form of wrath against sin. And He is at the same time the supreme and all-sufficient revelation to men of God's holy love in

its self-determination under the form of boundless grace even to the chief of sinners. The Person who has so revealed the love of God must be Divine.

313. *Fifth*, The Divinity of Christ becomes still further manifest in the light of *the power of His love over the hearts of men.* Before He died He said, "I, if I be lifted up from the earth, will draw all men unto me." When He uttered these, as when He uttered so many other words, He was conscious of being Divine. He felt that it would be His, as a personal right, to be the centre of spiritual power and attraction for all the members of the human race. But how was He to draw men? What was to be the nature of His power over them? It was to be the power of His holy, gracious love, especially as exercised and manifested on His cross. An instance of the fulfilment of His words and of the power of His love over the human heart is presented in Paul. He says, "I have been crucified with Christ, yet I live; and yet no longer I, but Christ liveth in me; and that life which I now live in the flesh, I live in faith, the faith which is in the Son of God who loved me, and gave Himself up for me." The words mean that he had been drawn to Christ by the power of His love as revealed in His cross. And the words as interpreted by his life show what the power of Christ's love effects when it wins the human heart as a sphere for its action. His love acts as a power effecting reconciliation between man as a sinner and God. It acts as a power effecting the personal redemption of man from sin. It acts as a power constraining the sinner consciously reconciled to God, with the power of sin broken in him, to surrender himself to Christ in a life of personal love and devotion. And it acts as a power in inspiring the heart with enthusiasm, and in filling the life with service for human beings. So Paul was drawn to Christ by the power of the love of Christ as lifted up on the cross. The effect of the power of Christ's love over his heart and life is typical. The effect corresponded with the cause. There was power in the cause to produce it. The same power has produced the same kind of manifold effect in the hearts and lives of

a countless multitude of others. The same power is acting in the hearts and lives of men to-day. Nor were there ever before so many hearts and lives of living persons in the world yielding to the drawing power of Christ's love. Christ's love as power is the most purifying, the most inspiring, the most elevating power in human life. It is what this power can do that every human life needs, and that is required by the entire body of human society. For all men to be drawn to Christ by the power of His love would be salvation; salvation to all men from every element of disturbance in the relations between the individual soul and God; and salvation from every element of disturbance between man and man. It is in the power of Christ's love to effect all this. But how could His love have such power if He Himself were not the eternal Son of God? We can form no higher conception of the nature and greatness of the love of God to the world than that which is presented in Christ. And we can conceive of Divine love as invested with no higher form of power than that which has been gained for it by the cross. We therefore conclude that Christ must be Divine. The question of His Divinity depends on nothing so much as on the question of His love; for God is love. Is Christ love? Is love the supreme characteristic of Christ? Is His love holy and gracious love? Is His love Divine love? Is it Divine in its nature, in its greatness, in its power? Is it not His love that reveals to men the perfect love of God? Then He must be Divine.

T. and T. Clark's Publications.

Handbooks for Bible Classes and Private Students.

Just published, in crown 8vo, price 1s. 6d.,

SERMONS,

BY THE RIGHT REVEREND FATHER IN GOD

JOSEPH BUTLER, D.C.L.,

LATE LORD BISHOP OF DURHAM.

SERMONS I., II., III.

UPON HUMAN NATURE, OR MAN CONSIDERED AS A MORAL AGENT.

Introduction and Notes

BY REV. THOMAS B. KILPATRICK, B.D.,

MINISTER AT FERRYHILL, ABERDEEN.

CONTENTS. — Introduction. — Biographical Sketch. — The Aim and Value of Ethical Study. — The Rise of Modern (British) Ethical Study: Thomas Hobbes. — Answers to Hobbes: Shaftesbury and Hutcheson. — Butler's Ethical Doctrine: Standpoint and Method: Statement: Estimate. — Concluding Remarks. — Text and Notes.

In crown 8vo, price 2s. 6d.,

PALESTINE:

ITS HISTORICAL GEOGRAPHY.

With Topographical Index.

BY REV. ARCHIBALD HENDERSON, M.A.

With Five Maps.

The Maps have been specially revised by Captain CONDER, R.E., of the Palestine Exploration Fund, for this Work.

'We cannot consider a Sunday-school teacher fully equipped without this volume.'—*Ecclesiastical Gazette.*

'It is exceedingly well written, and cannot fail to be a great boon to those for whom it is chiefly intended; while it must also be highly valuable to the general reader, embracing, as it does, most graphic descriptions of many of the scenes of ancient history, and of the stirring events of the times included in both the Old and the New Testament history.'—*Glasgow News.*

Handbooks for Bible Classes and Private Students.

EDITED BY

REV. MARCUS DODS, D.D.,

AND

REV. ALEXANDER WHYTE, D.D.

NOW READY.

THE EPISTLE TO THE GALATIANS. By JAMES MACGREGOR, D.D., late of New College, Edinburgh. *Price 1s. 6d.*

THE POST-EXILIAN PROPHETS. With Introductions and Notes. By Rev. MARCUS DODS, D.D., Glasgow. *Price 2s.*

A LIFE OF CHRIST. By Rev. JAMES STALKER, M.A. *Price 1s. 6d.*

THE SACRAMENTS. By Rev. Professor CANDLISH, D.D. *Price 1s. 6d.*

THE BOOKS OF CHRONICLES. By Rev. Professor MURPHY, LL.D., Belfast. *Price 1s. 6d.*

THE CONFESSION OF FAITH. By Rev. JOHN MACPHERSON, M.A., Findhorn. *Price 2s.*

THE BOOK OF JUDGES. By Rev. Principal DOUGLAS, D.D. *Price 1s. 3d.*

THE BOOK OF JOSHUA. By Rev. Principal DOUGLAS, D.D. *Price 1s. 6d.*

THE EPISTLE TO THE HEBREWS. By Rev. Professor DAVIDSON, D.D., Edinburgh. *Price 2s. 6d.*

SCOTTISH CHURCH HISTORY. By Rev. N. L. WALKER. *Price 1s. 6d.*

THE CHURCH. By Rev. Prof. BINNIE, D.D., Aberdeen. *Price 1s. 6d.*

THE REFORMATION. By Rev. Professor LINDSAY, D.D. *Price 2s.*

THE BOOK OF GENESIS. By Rev. MARCUS DODS, D.D. *Price 2s.*

THE EPISTLE TO THE ROMANS. By Rev. Principal BROWN, D.D., Aberdeen. *Price 2s.*

PRESBYTERIANISM. By Rev. JOHN MACPHERSON, M.A. *Price 1s. 6d.*

LESSONS ON THE LIFE OF CHRIST. By Rev. WM. SCRYMGEOUR, Glasgow. *Price 2s. 6d.*

THE SHORTER CATECHISM. By Rev. ALEXANDER WHYTE, D.D., Edinburgh. *Price 2s. 6d.*

THE GOSPEL ACCORDING TO ST. MARK. By Rev. Professor LINDSAY, D.D., Glasgow. *Price 2s. 6d.*

[Continued on next page.

HANDBOOKS FOR BIBLE CLASSES.

A SHORT HISTORY OF CHRISTIAN MISSIONS. By GEORGE SMITH, LL.D., F.R.G.S. *Price* 2s. 6d.

A LIFE OF ST. PAUL. By Rev. JAMES STALKER, M.A. *Price* 1s. 6d.

PALESTINE. With Maps. By Rev. ARCH. HENDERSON, M.A., Crieff. *Price* 2s. 6d.

THE BOOK OF ACTS. By Rev. Professor LINDSAY, D.D. Two Parts, *price* 1s. 6d. each.

THE WORK OF THE HOLY SPIRIT. By Rev. Professor CANDLISH. D.D. *Price* 1s. 6d.

THE SUM OF SAVING KNOWLEDGE. By Rev. JOHN MACPHERSON, M.A., Findhorn. *Price* 1s. 6d.

HISTORY OF THE IRISH PRESBYTERIAN CHURCH. By Rev. THOMAS HAMILTON, D.D., Belfast. *Price* 2s.

THE GOSPEL ACCORDING TO ST. LUKE. By Rev. Professor LINDSAY, M.A., D.D. Part I., *price* 2s. Part II., *price* 1s. 3d.

THE CHRISTIAN MIRACLES AND THE CONCLUSIONS OF SCIENCE. By Rev. W. D. THOMSON, M.A., Lochend. *Price* 2s.

BUTLER'S THREE SERMONS ON HUMAN NATURE. With Introduction and Notes. By Rev. T. B. KILPATRICK, B.D. *Price* 1s. 6d.

IN PREPARATION.

THE SABBATH. By Rev. Professor SALMOND, D.D., Aberdeen.

THE GOSPEL ACCORDING TO ST. JOHN. By Rev. GEORGE REITH, M.A., Glasgow. [*Shortly.*

THE FIRST EPISTLE TO THE CORINTHIANS. By Rev. MARCUS DODS, D.D., Glasgow.

THE SECOND EPISTLE TO THE CORINTHIANS. By Rev. Principal DAVID BROWN, D.D., Aberdeen.

THE EPISTLE TO THE PHILIPPIANS. By Rev. JAMES MELLIS, M.A., Southport.

THE EPISTLE TO THE COLOSSIANS. By Rev. SIMEON R. MACPHAIL, M.A., Liverpool.

CHURCH AND STATE. By A. TAYLOR INNES, Esq., Advocate, Edinburgh.

CHRISTIAN ETHICS. By Rev. Professor LINDSAY, D.D., Glasgow.

APOLOGETICS. By Rev. Professor IVERACH, M.A., Aberdeen.

THE BOOK OF EXODUS. By JAMES MACGREGOR, D.D., late of New College, Edinburgh.

THE DOCTRINE OF SIN. By Rev. Professor CANDLISH, D.D.

ISAIAH. By Rev. Professor ELMSLIE, M.A., London.

THE NEW TESTAMENT TIMES. By Rev. R. T. CUNNINGHAM, M.A., Bowdon.

T. and T. Clark's Publications.

HERZOG'S
BIBLICAL ENCYCLOPÆDIA.

Now complete, in Three Vols. imp. 8vo, price 24s. each,

ENCYCLOPÆDIA OR DICTIONARY
OF
Biblical, Historical, Doctrinal, and Practical Theology.

Based on the Real-Encyclopädie of Herzog, Plitt, and Hauck.

EDITED BY PHILIP SCHAFF, D.D., LL.D.

'A well designed, meritorious work, on which neither industry nor expense has been spared.'—*Guardian.*

'This certainly is a remarkable work. . . . It will be one without which no general or theological or biographical library will be complete.'—*Freeman.*

'The need of such a work as this must be very often felt, and it ought to find its way into all college libraries, and into many private studies.'—*Christian World.*

'As a comprehensive work of reference, within a moderate compass, we know nothing at all equal to it in the large department which it deals with.—*Church Bells.*

Now complete, in Four Vols. imp. 8vo, price 12s. 6d. each,

COMMENTARY ON THE NEW TESTAMENT.
With Illustrations and Maps.

EDITED BY PHILIP SCHAFF, D.D., LL.D.

Volume I.	*Volume II.*
THE SYNOPTICAL GOSPELS.	ST. JOHN'S GOSPEL AND THE ACT OF THE APOSTLES.
Volume III.	*Volume IV.*
ROMANS to PHILEMON.	HEBREWS to REVELATION.

'A useful, valuable, and instructive commentary The interpretation is set forth with clearness and cogency, and in a manner calculated to commend the volumes to the thoughtful reader. The book is beautifully got up, and reflects great credit on the publishers as well as the writers.'—*The Bishop of Gloucester.*

'There are few better commentaries having a similar scope and object; indeed, within the same limits, we do not know of one so good upon the whole of the New Testament.'—*Literary World.*

'External beauty and intrinsic worth combine in the work here completed. Good paper, good type, good illustrations, good binding, please the eye, as accuracy and thoroughness in matter of treatment satisfy the judgment. Everywhere the workmanship is careful, solid, harmonious.'—*Methodist Recorder.*

T. and T. Clark's Publications.

LOTZE'S MICROCOSMUS.

Just published, Second Edition, in Two Vols., 8vo, price 36s.,

MICROCOSMUS:
CONCERNING MAN AND HIS RELATION TO THE WORLD.

By HERMANN LOTZE.

CONTENTS:—Book I. The Body. II. The Soul. III. Life. IV. Man. V. Mind. VI. The Microcosmic Order; or, The Course of Human Life. VII. History. VIII. Progress. IX. The Unity of Things.

'These are indeed two masterly volumes, vigorous in intellectual power, and translated with rare ability. . . . This work will doubtless find a place on the shelves of all the foremost thinkers and students of modern times.'—*Evangelical Magazine.*

'The English public have now before them the greatest philosophic work produced in Germany by the generation just past. The translation comes at an opportune time, for the circumstances of English thought just at the present moment are peculiarly those with which Lotze attempted to deal when he wrote his "Microcosmus" a quarter of a century ago. . . . Few philosophic books of the century are so attractive both in style and matter.'—*Athenæum.*

'Lotze is the ablest, the most brilliant, and most renowned of the German philosophers of to-day. . . . He has rendered invaluable and splendid service to Christian thinkers, and has given them a work which cannot fail to equip them for the sturdiest intellectual conflicts and to ensure their victory.'—*Baptist Magazine.*

In Two Vols., 8vo, price 21s.,

NATURE AND THE BIBLE:
LECTURES ON THE MOSAIC HISTORY OF CREATION IN ITS RELATION TO NATURAL SCIENCE.

By Dr. FR. H. REUSCH.

REVISED AND CORRECTED BY THE AUTHOR.

Translated from the Fourth Edition

By KATHLEEN LYTTELTON.

'Other champions much more competent and learned than myself might have been placed in the field; I will only name one of the most recent, Dr. Reusch, author of "Nature and the Bible."'—The Right Hon. W. E. GLADSTONE.

'The work, we need hardly say, is of profound and perennial interest, and it can scarcely be too highly commended as, in many respects, a very successful attempt to settle one of the most perplexing questions of the day. It is impossible to read it without obtaining larger views of theology, and more accurate opinions respecting its relations to science, and no one will rise from its perusal without feeling a deep sense of gratitude to its author.'—*Scottish Review.*

T. and T. Clark's Publications.

Just published, in crown 8vo, price 3s. 6d., SECOND EDITION, REVISED,

THE THEOLOGY AND THEOLOGIANS OF SCOTLAND,

CHIEFLY OF THE

Seventeenth and Eighteenth Centuries.

Being one of the 'Cunningham Lectures.'

BY JAMES WALKER, D.D., CARNWATH.

CONTENTS.—CHAP. I. Survey of the Field. II. Predestination and Providence. III. The Atonement. IV. The Doctrine of the Visible Church. V. The Headship of Christ and Erastianism. VI. Present Misrepresentation of Scottish Religion. VII. Do Presbyterians hold Apostolical Succession?

'These pages glow with fervent and eloquent rejoinder to the cheap scorn and scurrilous satire poured out upon evangelical theology as it has been developed north of the Tweed.'—*British Quarterly Review.*

'We do not wonder that in their delivery Dr. Walker's lectures excited great interest; we should have wondered far more if they had not done so.'— Mr. SPURGEON in *Sword and Trowel.*

'As an able and eloquent vindication of Scottish theology, the work is one of very great interest—an interest by no means necessarily confined to theologians. The history of Scotland, and the character of her people, cannot be understood without an intelligent and sympathetic study of her theology, and in this Dr. Walker's little book will be found to render unique assistance.'—*Scotsman.*

Just published, in crown 8vo, price 5s.,

THE VOICE FROM THE CROSS:

A Series of Sermons on our Lord's Passion

BY EMINENT LIVING PREACHERS OF GERMANY,

INCLUDING

Rev. Drs. AHLFELD, BAUR, BAYER, COUARD, FABER, FROMMEL, GEROK, HÄRNELT, HANSEN, KÖGEL, LUTHARDT, MÜHE, MÜLLENSIEFEN, NEBE, QUANDT, SCHRADER, SCHRÖTER, STÖCKER, AND TEICHMÜLLER.

WITH BIOGRAPHICAL SKETCHES,

AND PORTRAIT OF DR. KÖGEL.

Edited and Translated by William Macintosh, M.A., F.S.S.

www.ingramcontent.com/pod-product-compliance
Lightning Source LLC
Chambersburg PA
CBHW031447160426
43195CB00010BB/892